Honduras

Toward Better Health Care for All

The World Bank
Washington, D.C.

World Bank Country Studies are among the many reports originally prepared for internal use as part of the continuing analysis by the Bank of the economic and related conditions of its developing member countries and of its dialogues with the governments. Some of the reports are published in this series with the least possible delay for the use of governments and the academic, business and financial, and development communities. The typescript of this paper therefore has not been prepared in accordance with the procedures appropriate to formal printed texts, and the World Bank accepts no responsibility for errors. Some sources cited in this paper may be informal documents that are not readily available.

The findings, interpretations, and conclusions expressed in this paper are entirely those of the author(s) and should not be attributed in any manner to the World Bank, to its affiliated organizations, or to members of its Board of Executive Directors or the countries they represent. The World Bank does not guarantee the accuracy of the data included in this publication and accepts no responsibility for any consequence of their use. The boundaries, colors, denominations, and other information shown on any map in this volume do not imply on the part of the World Bank Group any judgment on the legal status of any territory or the endorsement or acceptance of such boundaries.

The material in this publication is copyrighted. Requests for permission to reproduce portions of it should be sent to the Office of the Publisher at the address shown in the copyright notice above. The World Bank encourages dissemination of its work and will normally give permission promptly and, when the reproduction is for noncommercial purposes, without asking a fee. Permission to copy portions for classroom use is granted through the Copyright Clearance Center, Inc., Suite 910, 222 Rosewood Drive, Danvers, Massachusetts 01923, U.S.A.

ISSN: 0253-2123

Library of Congress Cataloging-in-Publication Data

Honduras : toward better health care for all.
     p.   cm. — (A World Bank country study, ISSN 0253-2123)
  ISBN 0-8213-4190-1
  1. Health planning—Honduras. 2. Medical care—Honduras.
3. Honduras—Statistics, Medical. I. World Bank. II. Series.
RA395.H6H67   1998
362.1'097283—dc21
                                            98-11111
                                            CIP

ABSTRACT

This report was prepared by the World Bank as a contribution to its ongoing policy dialogue with the Government of Honduras. It is based on the results of a mission that visited Honduras in April 1997 and worked in collaboration with Government officials from the Ministry of Health, the Ministry of Finance, the Commission for the Modernization of the State, the Social Security Institute, donors involved in the health sector and private sector representatives.

The report was prepared at the request of the Government with three objectives:
- to serve the administration inaugurated in 1998 as an input to design a policy for the health sector aiming to ensure continuity with past efforts to increase access by the poor to the health sector. The new health sector policy should also serve as an instrument for improved donor coordination;
- to facilitate a dialogue between the Economic Cabinet, concerned with perceived inefficiencies in the use of public funds and in the effectiveness of externally-financed programs and the authorities responsible for the social sectors, concerned with equity and safety; and
- to define possible IDA support for the health sector.

The report begins by describing the achievements in improving the health status of the population over the past three decades and the challenges for the next decade. There have been important achievements, but several features of the health sector introduce a note of caution to the overall optimism of the report: the divorce between primary clinics and hospitals; the primary health network's dependence on donors; and a past history of vulnerability to internal and external pressures. The report discusses the challenges that need to be faced to modernize public sector financing, to improve public sector provision and to develop an appropriate policy and regulatory framework for pharmaceuticals and social security.

ACRONYMS AND ABBREVIATIONS

AMIHSS	Asociación de Médicos del Instituto de Seguro Social
CEFASA	Censo Familiar de Salud (Family Health Census)
CENARH	Centro Nacional de Adiestramiento de Recursos Humanos (National Training Center)
CESAMO	Centro de Salud con Médico (Health Clinic with Doctor)
CESAR	Centro de Salud Rural (Rural Health Clinic)
CMI	Clínica Materno Infantil (Birthing Center)
CNTS	Coordinadora Nacional de los Trabajadores de la Salud (National Health Workers Union)
EMRP	Fondo de Enfermedad, Maternidad y Riesgo Profesional (Sickness, Maternity and Professional Risk Fund)
FHIS	Fondo Hondureño de Inversión Social (Honduran Social Investment Fund)
GDP	Gross Domestic Product
IDA	International Development Agency
IDB	InterAmerican Development Bank
IHSS	Instituto Hondureño de Seguridad Social (Honduran Social Security Institute)
IMF	International Monetary Fund
IRA	Infecciones Respiratorias Agudas (Acute Respiratory Infections)
JICA	Japanese International Cooperation Agency
LAC	Latin America and the Caribbean
LME	Ley del Empleado Médico (Law on the Employment of Doctors)
MOF	Ministry of Finance
MSP	Ministerio de Salud Pública (Ministry of Public Health)
NGO	Non Governmental Organization
NHES	National Health Expenditure Survey of 1995
PAHO	Pan-American Health Organization
RUD	Rational use of drugs
SIAF	Sistema de Información de Administración Financiera (Financial Management Information System)
SIGAF	Sistema de Información Gerencial Administrativo-Financiera (Administrative and Financial Management Information System)
SITRAIHSS	Sindicato de Trabajadores del IHSS (Union of IHSS Workers)
SITRAMEDYS	Sindicato de Trabajadores de Medicina y Similares (Health Sector Union)
STD	Sexual Transmissible Diseases
TB	Tuberculosis
UNAH	Universidad Autónoma de Honduras (National Autonomous University)
UNDP	United Nations Development Program
UNICEF	United Nations Children's Fund
UPS	Unidad Productora de Servicios de Salud (Public Health Providers)
WHO	World Health Organization

GOVERNMENT FISCAL YEAR
January 1 - December 31

CURRENCY EQUIVALENTS
Currency Unit = Lempira
$1.00 = L9.43 (Average for 1995)

Vice President	:	Shahid Javed Burki
Country Director	:	Donna Dowsett-Coirolo
Sector Director	:	Julian Schweitzer
Sector Specialist	:	Xavier Coll
Task Manager	:	Daniel Cotlear

CONTENTS

This report is based on the findings of a World Bank mission that visited Honduras in April of 1997. The mission was integrated by Daniel Cotlear (team leader and main author of this report), Ian Walker (co-author of the equity estimations and the chapters on co-payments and efficiency and editor); Veerle Coignez-Sterling (pharmaceuticals), Rony Lenz (financial administration and social security), Carlos Daniel Pinheiro (epidemiological profile), Fidel Ordóñez (data processing) and Helmis Cardenas (initial draft of the National Health Accounts and general mission support). Peer reviewers were Maureen Lewis, William Mcgreevey and Dominique van de Walle. Shahid Javed Burki is Vice President. Donna Dowsett-Coirolo is Country Director. Ana-Maria Arriagada is Country Sector Leader. Ian Bannon is Lead Economist. Xavier Coll is Lead Health Specialist.

TABLES

DIAGRAMS

TEXT BOXES

EXECUTIVE SUMMARY

Honduras may be justly proud of its achievements in improving the health status of its population over the last three decades. After exhibiting in the 1960s an infant mortality rate (IMR) 50% worse than the Latin American average, it reduced infant mortality at a faster pace than most of its neighbors, reaching in 1995, the average for Latin America, and surpassing in the process Bolivia, Brazil, Guatemala, Nicaragua and Peru. These achievements are the result of a combination of economic development, improved education, increased access to safe water, and a large effort to improve basic health programs. The new estimate of total health expenditure, at 7.2% of GDP, is higher than was suggested by previous studies, which have tended to underplay the importance of private expenditure on health which accounts for more than half of the total. Funding from external agencies has been very large in recent years, accounting for half of the expenditures of the primary care network. The substantial resources assigned to mother and child health, and the resulting relatively high degree of concentration of public expenditures in health on the poor has placed Honduras well ahead of many of its richer neighbors in terms of access to basic services.

However, Honduras cannot afford to rest on its laurels. Its achievements are the result of what may be considered a first stage in the development of its health system, consisting of a considerable physical expansion of health care facilities and the establishment of essential elements for the provision of key basic services. The Administration that will take office in 1998 will need to advance to a second stage where the role of the Government will be more complex. The challenge for the second stage is to sustain and deepen the achievements in primary health care within a fragile institutional environment, while responding to the growing pressure for additional clinical services from an increasingly urban and better educated population. The poor increasingly demand services such as maternal care (two thirds of births in rural areas are still home-based), and better quality in the treatment of injuries and of basic surgery. The middle class demands more high-tech services and, faced with an inoperative social security system, lobbies the Government for cheap public provision of those high-end services. These new demands are compounded by the challenges that accompany population growth and urbanization and by the very high incidence of AIDS in certain parts of the country.

Three features of the health sector make it fragile and introduce a note of caution to the overall optimism of this report. First, there is a deep divorce between the operation of the hospitals and the primary health clinics, whereas the improvement in the health status of the poor described in this report is based primarily on the expansion and improved operation of the clinics. Second, the primary health network is dependent on donor financing and on donor-managed institutional arrangements. Third, the insufficiently examined approval of a large supplier loan for hospital equipment,

combined with continued pressures for the rushed approval of additional loans and large wage increases in the final months of the Reina Administration suggest the imminent risk of a repetition of the mistakes of the 1970s, when the Government ceded control over its investment program to interest groups allowing an unplanned growth of the hospital sector. The disproportionate weight of hospitals in public expenditures during the 1980s was only reversed in the last decade by increasing the overall fiscal effort assigned to the health sector and by recourse to the abundant external finance.

This report is produced as an input to be used by the new Administration to develop a vision for the sector. The report discusses the challenges that need to be faced to modernize public sector financing, to improve public sector service provision and to develop an appropriate policy and regulatory framework for pharmaceuticals and social security.

Modernizing public sector financing

Financial management in MSP is highly centralized, rigid and traditional. Five problems areas are discussed in the report: (i) many donors support MSP as a service provider, but do not entrust its bureaucracy with the funds, making the budget a less effective tool for fiscal control and sectoral planning; (ii) the budgetary system provides no incentives for improved performance as it allocates resources on the basis of past allocations, without reference to a forward-looking planning process and without adjustments based on past performance; (iii) regional directors have little influence over the design and management of the budget of the hospitals in their region; (iv) rigidity of budgetary execution; and (v) accounting, cost measurement and information systems weaknesses. Modernizing MSP's financial management requires changes in its organizational structure and procedures, complemented by a large investment in capacity building. Urgent reforms include: (i) fine-tune MSP's 1997 reorganization to separate the functions of financing and sectoral planning, regulation of health services, and direct service provision; (ii) consolidate regionalization by constituting health regions as autonomous public entities and giving regional directors responsibility for managing all establishments (including area hospitals) and programs in their region; (iii) modernize the MSP budget through payment-by-results by establishing management contracts between MSP and autonomous health regions, agreeing on specific monitorable objectives within an established system of rewards and penalties; and (iv) make MSP budget execution more flexible.

Although MSP has charged its users for services for 20 years, co-payments remain highly controversial. Co-payment income covers only 1.5% to 3.5% of the total MSP budget. Nevertheless, the funds are important because they constitute liquid resources, free from bureaucratic procedures. There is little evidence to support the claim that co-payments undermine access for the poor as charges are very low relative to incomes, even for the poor. Prices for basic services are under 5% of what the private sector charges for the same service and they are normally waived when the patient cannot pay. The real problems with co-payments are that as presently operated, the

system creates problems of equity and efficiency as it: (i) provides insufficient checks on the consumption of highly subsidized tertiary hospital treatments by the non-poor; (ii) gives incentives to hospitals and health centers to over-expand cash producing services; and (iii) sends irrational price signals to MSP clients about where to seek attention.

Co-payments play an important role in most modern systems of health financing. They give economic signals that guide the efficient use of resources, they discourage unnecessary care and they promote equity by limiting misdirected subsidies. In Honduras co-payments are not and should not be meant to recover the full costs of producing health services as this would be incompatible with equity of access. The Government should re-establish the legitimacy of co-payments by making a clear statement of the system's objectives and by rationalizing its rules. A special policy should be designed for high cost hospital interventions eliminating public subsidies for beneficiaries of social security and of private insurance. A fund should be created to subsidize those who cannot afford to pay.

Improving the public provision of services

Between 1990-96, the number of area hospitals increased by 129%, and rural clinics by 41%. In the same period, total consultations grew substantially less, suggesting that expansion has been associated with growing underutilization of facilities. Average productivity in the primary network is low. In 1996, CESARs (clinics staffed by auxiliary nurses) averaged just 6 consultations per nurse-day. Only 19% of CESAMOs reach the benchmark of 36 consultations per doctor-day recommended by the *Colegio Médico*. These low utilization levels result in high costs. Remarkably, the unit cost of an ambulatory consultation in an MSP hospital is similar to that for the ambulatory clinics, in spite of the higher qualifications and overhead cost of the hospital staff. Most health centers are located in areas of relatively high population density. The main causes of health center underutilization are: oversupply created as a result of the divorce in the operations of hospitals and primary clinics which often leads to needless duplication and lack of demand resulting from frequent closures, long waiting times, short opening hours and poor service quality due to medicines in short supply, frequent closure of laboratories and a low resolution capacity of the staff. Productivity in hospitals is also low, especially in area hospitals.

The report makes recommendations to improve utilization and productivity. For health clinics: implement a permanent system of monitoring utilization, develop regional teams and give them the authority within the new decentralization framework to tackle the problems identified, and strengthen hospital-health center collaboration, starting with a pilot program for reorganizing local health services. For hospitals: re-think the role of underutilized area hospitals. In some cases it may be appropriate to consider turning them into birthing and emergency centers and reducing the required number of specialists accordingly; find ways to make full use of MSP hospitals in the afternoons, some options that may gain support from the physicians and nurses are suggested in the main report; as part of MSP administrative decentralization, hospitals should be given their own budgets for the purchase, operation and maintenance of equipment.

Together with the budgetary, financial and pricing problems discussed above, labor market problems are one of the main sources of inefficiency in the health system. In relation to its income, Honduras, is relatively well endowed with doctors but it has one of the lowest ratios of professional nurses in the continent. MSP has become by far the most important employer of medical professionals after increasing its employment of physicians by 30% and of professional nurses by 115% during the current Administration. Training of nurses and doctors is publicly funded through the National Autonomous University (UNAH) and suffers from many and costly inefficiencies. The labor market is heavily influenced by the presence of unions and the doctors' professional body, and by complex labor legislation, including, importantly, the *Ley del Médico Empleado* that regulates employment of physicians. This institutional framework has created rigidities that contribute to: the concentration of doctors and nurses in major cities, the underutilization of hospitals and CESAMOs in the afternoons, and the selection of inadequate staff for key managerial positions. These issues are not unique to Honduras, and many countries are struggling to reform their training systems and to introduce more flexibility to their labor markets. This is nowhere an easy task and it is one that takes time, as it needs to be implemented with consensus. Honduras has been slower than many of its neighbors to begin to confront labor market issues and it is time to begin to bring these issues into the policy agenda.

First, the Government and the University need to work together and produce a strategy for training of health sector staff. Key issues that need to be addressed include: the opening of a specialization in general family medicine as a basis for high quality attention outside a hospital environment; the implementation of measures to reduce the high drop out rate for doctors and professional nurses; developing specialized management training programs and raising the supply of professional nurses. Second, a reform of the pay systems is needed. In particular, in view of the large salary increases being requested by the *Colegio Médico* in the run-up to the elections, this might be the right time for a public debate linking pay increases with the increased flexibility needed to improve the quality and access to MSP services. Some desirable changes include: improve the pay of professional nurses and other auxiliary staff to solve the problems of recruiting and retaining high quality personnel at that level; increase zoning payments to resolve regional staffing problems -- only physicians can be given zoning payments, and these are capped at low levels and are available for few areas; link future pay increases to specific gains in productivity, to reassignment from morning to afternoon and evening shifts and to quality indicators (including length of wait by patients). A third crucial area in need of reform is the criteria for the appointment of staff to managerial positions. The use of political appointees should be abandoned, and managerial skills should become the overriding selection criteria for these position.

Developing policies for pharmaceuticals and social security

The early 1990s saw significant improvements in pharmaceuticals policy with the approval of the Health Code and a substantial liberalization of the sector. But the sector's great economic and medical importance means that it will continue to require the Government's priority attention. Pharmaceutical expenditures amount to almost 3% of GDP, most of which is spent by households in private pharmacies for self-medication. The three main challenges for policy makers today are: (i) the continued drug shortage in MSP health centers and hospitals; (ii) MSP's weaknesses in regulatory and enforcement capacity especially in the area of pharmaceutical quality assurance; and (iii) the need to improve the rational use of drugs (RUD).

Improving drug availability in the public sector will require changes in the supply chain and in pricing policy. In the supply chain there is a need for: (i) training to improve inventory management; (ii) strengthening distribution with a combination of selective investments and the use of private services; and (iii) continue to improve procurement by opening public procurement to international competition and adopting a less controlist combination of centralized and decentralized procurement to balance the economies of scale obtained by centralized purchases with the greater timeliness and local choice of decentralized purchases. The pricing policy for drugs also requires consideration. Drugs are free in the public sector, but are often not available. In urban areas patients purchase their drugs from pharmacies. In rural areas patients increasingly purchase their drugs from communal pharmacies (*Fondos Comunales*) which have rapidly developed with support from NGOs and are now approved by MSP. Honduras should consider replicating the experience of other countries which, faced with similar conditions, have brought the *Fondos Comunales* into the public health centers, replacing their inoperative public pharmacies. This policy could be supplemented by focusing the subsidy in the free distribution of a more limited number of selected vital drugs.

The main regulatory weaknesses require a technical response and some reforms. Strengthening MSP's technical capacity, especially in the area of quality assurance, requires training and crucially, improving the pay and the professional prospects for the staff to stop the drain of capacity and expertise to the more lucrative private sector. Two issues require reform. First, to guarantee objectivity, the national laboratory should be made independent of the professional body of the pharmacists (*Colegio Químico-Farmacéutico*). Second, over the long run, great benefits could arise from Central American integration, by mutual recognition of registration, by developing a regional quality control network and by a common marketing authorization agency.

Finally, to enhance the rational use of drugs, MSP should: accelerate the adoption of WHO's "Ethical Criteria for Drug Promotion"; work with UNAH to emphasize RUD in the curriculum of medical and pharmacy studies and work with the *Colegio Médico* to implement RUD training programs for physicians.

The Honduran social security system (IHSS) is one of the least developed in Latin America, covering no more than 10% of the population. Most beneficiaries are concentrated in Tegucigalpa and San Pedro Sula where the three hospitals that absorb the lion's share of IHSS health budget are located. IHSS is in a vicious circle in which poor performance has led to private sector resistance to increased funding and the resulting budgetary crisis feeds back into still worse performance. The effective contribution to social security is made minuscule due to an income ceiling which has been frozen for 30 years and limits on the maximum monthly contribution per insured worker to the health and maternity fund to just $3. For many years, the resulting deficit of the health fund has been financed by squeezing the pension fund which is managed jointly with the health fund. In recent years, the private sector and Congress have refused to increase the income ceiling ("until the waste is eliminated in the hospitals"). The IHSS administration has responded to the financial crisis by cutting to the bone discretionary expenditures on items such as drugs, medical materials, investment and maintenance. While wages and salaries have remained stable in real terms. This has resulted in a crisis of performance. IHSS is less efficient than MSP, in physical and in cost terms, with higher costs due to overstaffing, high administrative costs and low utilization of beds.

The crisis of IHSS is so deep that it is unlikely that the institution can become efficient without structural changes. Management consultants looking at the financial position of IHSS and at the needs of the pension fund invariably recommend raising the ceilings for the calculation of contributions, and separating the pensions fund from the health fund. These are necessary measures, but are not enough as they leave unsolved the problems of efficiency of service delivery. The main recommendation of this report is that in addition to those measures the reform should focus on strengthening the role of IHSS as public insurer and end its role as a direct service provider. To achieve this, there needs to be a separation in the ownership and administration of the health network from the administration of the health insurance. This could be done by creating a separate autonomous entity to run the health network; by passing the hospitals and clinics to MSP, by privatizing them, or by a combination of these. This separation is a key element of the proposed reform, required to allow IHSS to focus on its role as insurer and abandon its traditional focus on the supply of health services. The main report elaborates on additional reform and capacity building measures that would be necessary to give new life to IHSS. An important message of the report is that the reform of IHSS is needed not just for the sake of IHSS, but also to avoid the build up of pressures over MSP to deliver high end services.

RESUMEN EJECUTIVO

Es justo que Honduras vea con orgullo lo que ha logrado en materia de mejora de la salud de su población en las últimas tres décadas. Luego de exhibir en la década de los años sesenta, un índice de mortalidad infantil un 50 por ciento peor que el promedio de América Latina, fue capaz de reducir la mortalidad infantil (IMI) mucho más rápido que la mayoría de sus vecinos, alcanzando en 1995 el promedio correspondiente a América Latina y sobrepasando en su trayecto, a las cifras correspondientes a Bolivia, Brasil, Nicaragua y Perú. Estos logros son el resultado de una combinación de desarrollo económico, mejoras en la educación, aumento del acceso al agua potable, y un gran esfuerzo por mejorar los programas básicos de salud. La nueva cifra estimada de gastos totales en la salud, situada en el 7,2 por ciento del PBI, es más alta que aquélla sugerida por los estudios realizados anteriormente que han tendido a restar importancia a los gastos privados en la salud, los cuales corresponden a más de la mitad de dicho total. El financiamiento proveniente de agencias externas ha sido muy elevado en los últimos años, atribuyéndoseles a éstas la mitad de los gastos de la red de cuidados primarios. Los sustanciales recursos asignados a la salud materno-infantil, y el grado relativamente alto de gastos públicos en la salud que se han concentrado en la población pobre, ha ubicado a Honduras muy por delante de muchos de sus vecinos más ricos en términos de acceso a servicios básicos.

No obstante, Honduras no puede darse el lujo de dormir en sus laureles. Estos logros son el resultado de lo que podría considerarse una primera etapa en el desarrollo de su sistema de salud, consistente en una considerable expansión física de sus centros de salud y el establecimiento de elementos esenciales para la provisión de servicios básicos clave. La Administración que habrá de asumir el gobierno en 1998 necesitará avanzar hacia una segunda etapa, donde el papel desempeñado por el Gobierno será más complejo. El desafío para la segunda etapa será mantener y profundizar los logros concretados en materia de cuidados primarios dentro de un medio institucional frágil, respondiendo al mismo tiempo a una creciente demanda por servicios clínicos adicionales de una población cada vez más urbanizada y mejor educada. Entre la población pobre, existe una demanda cada vez mayor por servicios como los de cuidado maternal (dos tercios de los nacimientos en áreas rurales son aún en los hogares) y de mejor calidad en los tratamientos de heridas y cirugía básica. La clase media demanda más servicios de alta tecnología y, frente a un sistema de seguridad social inoperativo, ejerce presión sobre el Gobierno para que éste invierta en equipos especializados y subsidie servicios sofisticados. Estas nuevas demandas se ven particularmente agravadas por los desafíos propios del crecimiento y la urbanización de la población, así como la elevada incidencia del SIDA en algunas partes del país.

Tres aspectos del sector de la salud lo hacen frágil e introducen una nota de precaución al optimismo general de este informe. En primer lugar, existe una profunda separación entre la operación de los hospitales y de las clínicas de cuidados primarios, y las mejoras logradas en la situación de la salud de la población pobre que se describen en el presente informe, están basadas principalmente en la mejor operación y expansión de las clínicas. En segundo lugar, la red primaria depende en importante medida del financiamiento de donantes y de arreglos institucionales administrados por donantes. En tercer lugar, la aprobación insuficientemente analizada, de un préstamo de un proveedor para la compra de equipo hospitalario, conjuntamente con las continuas presiones por una aprobación rápida de préstamos adicionales e incrementos salariales significativos en los últimos meses de la Administración Reina, sugieren un inminente riesgo de repetir los errores cometidos en la década de los años setenta, cuando el gobierno cedió el control de su programa de inversión a grupos de interés que permitieron un crecimiento imprevisto del sector hospitalario. La desproporción del peso que adquirieron los hospitales en el gasto público en la década de los años ochenta, se pudo balancear recien en los últimos años y requirió un fuerte incremento del gasto fiscal asignado al sector de la salud e hizo uso de abundante financiamiento externo.

El presente informe ha sido producido como un insumo a ser utilizado por la nueva Administración, para desarrollar una estrategia para el sector. El informe analiza los desafios que será necesario enfrentar para modernizar al financiamiento del sector público, para mejorar la provisión de servicios del sector público y para desarrollar una política apropiada así como un marco regulador para la industria farmacéutica y la seguridad social.

La modernización del financiamiento del sector público

La administración financiera en el MSP es altamente centralizada, rígida y tradicional. El informe analiza cinco áreas problemáticas: (i) muchos donantes apoyan al MSP como un proveedor de servicios, pero no le confian los fondos a su burocracia, lo cual hace que el presupuesto constituya un instrumento de control fiscal y planificación sectorial menos efectivo; (ii) el sistema presupuestal no ofrece incentivos para un mejor rendimiento, dado que asigna recursos en base a asignaciones anteriores, sin referencia alguna a un proceso de planificación enfocado hacia el futuro y sin ajustes en base al rendimiento registrado en el pasado; (iii) los directores regionales poseen poca influencia sobre el diseño y el manejo de los presupuestos en los hospitales de sus regiones; (iv) la rigidez de su ejecución presupuestaria; y (v) los puntos débiles de los sistemas informáticos y de medición de costos y contabilidad. La modernización de la administración financiera del MSP requiere de cambios en sus procedimientos y estructura orgánica, complementados también por una gran inversión en el aumento de su capacidad. Entre las reformas más urgentes, se incluyen: (i) refinar la reorganización de 1997 del MSP, de manera de separar las funciones de: financiamiento y planificación sectorial, regulación de servicios sanitarios, y la provisión de servicios directos; (ii) consolidar la regionalización mediante la formación de regiones sanitarias como entes autónomos públicos y adjudicando a los directores regionales la responsabilidad por la administración de todos los establecimientos (incluyendo los hospitales del área) y programas de sus respectivas regiones; (iii) modernizar el presupuesto del MSP a través de pagos-de-acuerdo-a-resultados acordados mediante contratos de gestión entre el MSP y las regiones sanitarias autónomas, llegando a un acuerdo con respecto a objetivos específicos dentro de un sistema establecido de premios y sanciones; y (iv) flexibilizar la ejecución del presupuesto del MSP.

Aunque el MSP ha cobrado a sus usuarios por los servicios prestados durante 20 años, los copagos continúan siendo motivo de gran controversia. Los ingresos por concepto de copagos cubren únicamente entre el 1,5 y el 3,5 por ciento del presupuesto total del MSP, sin embargo, estos fondos son importantes debido a que constituyen recursos líquidos, libres de procesos burocráticos. Existe muy poca evidencia que apoye la teoría de que los copagos terminan por socavar el acceso para la población pobre, ya que los cargos son muy bajos en relación a los ingresos, aún para la población pobre. Los precios por servicios básicos se sitúan en un cinco por ciento menos de lo que cobra el sector privado por el mismo servicio, y normalmente se exime de dichos cargos a los pacientes que no los pueden pagar. Los verdaderos problemas de los copagos, radican en el hecho de que el sistema, tal como opera en el presente, crea problemas de equidad y eficiencia, ya que: (i) ofrece insuficiente desincentivos al consumo de tratamientos hospitalarios sofisticados altamente subsidiados de la población pudiente; (ii) otorga incentivos a hospitales y centros de salud para la sobreproducción de servicios a traves de los cuales obtienen liquidez; y (iii) envía señales de precios irracionales a usuarios del MSP con respecto a dónde buscar atención.

Los copagos desempeñan un papel importante en la mayoría de los sistemas modernos de financiamiento de sistemas de salud. Los mismos dan señales económicas que sirven de guía para un uso eficiente de los recursos, desalientan cuidados innecesarios, y promueven la equidad limitando el uso de subsidios maldirigidos. En Honduras, los copagos no tienen ni deben tener como misión la de recuperar la totalidad de los costos de la producción de servicios sanitarios, ya que esto sería incompatible con una equidad de acceso. El Gobierno debiera reestablecer la legitimidad de los copagos manifestando claramente los objetivos del sistema y racionalizando sus normas. Se deberá diseñar una política especial para atender a las intervenciones hospitalarias de alto costo, eliminando los subsidios públicos para los beneficiarios de la seguridad social y de seguros privados, y creando un fondo para subvencionar a aquéllos que no pueden pagar estos montos.

La modernización en la provisión de servicios públicos

Entre 1990-96, la cantidad de hospitales de área aumentó un 129 por ciento, y las clínicas rurales un 41 por ciento. Durante el mismo período, el total de consultas aumentó sustancialmente menos, lo que sugiere que la expansión estuvo asociada a una creciente subutilización de instalaciones. La productividad promedio en la red primaria es baja. En 1996, los CESARs (clínicas cuyo personal se compone de auxiliares de enfermería) tuvieron un promedio de apenas seis consultas por enfermera por día. Solamente el 19 por ciento de los CESAMOs alcanzan la cifra de referencia de 36 consultas por médico por día, recomendada por el *Colegio Médico*. Estos bajos niveles de utilización tienen como resultado costos altos. Llamativamente, el costo unitario de una consulta ambulante en un hospital del MSP es similar a aquél de clínicas ambulatorias, a pesar de requerir el primero calificaciones más especializadas y tener costos fijos más elevados. La mayoría de los centros de salud se encuentran ubicados en áreas con una densidad de población relativamente alta. Las principales causas de la subutilización de los centros de salud son: (i) la sobreoferta creada a raíz del divorcio entre las operaciones de hospitales y de clínicas primarias, que a menudo conduce a una duplicación innecesaria de infraestructura y (ii) la carencia de demanda resultante de una percepción negativa de la calidad del servicio de las clínicas debida a cierres frecuentes, períodos de espera prolongados, horarios de operación reducidos, desabastecimiento de medicinas, frecuente cierre de laboratorios, y capacidad de resolución limitada del personal. La productividad en hospitales es también baja, en particular en los hospitales de área.

El informe presenta recomendaciones para mejorar la utilización y la productividad. En el caso de las clínicas sería recomendable implementar un sistema per-manente de monitoreo de su utilización, desarrollar equipos regionales y proporcionarles autoridad dentro del nuevo marco de descentralización de manera de atacar a los problemas identificados, y fortalecer la colaboración entre los centros de salud y los hospitales, comenzando con un programa piloto para reorganizar a los servicios sanitarios locales. En el caso de los hospitales, se recomienda volver a evaluar el papel de los hospitales de área subutilizados; en algunos casos podría ser apropiado considerar su conversión en clínicas materno-infantiles y de emergencia, y reducir la cantidad de especialistas de manera acorde. Otro reto importante es encontrar formas de utilizar plenamente a los hospitales del MSP en las tardes. En el informe se sugieren algunas opciones que podrían contar con el apoyo de médicos y enfermeras. Tercero, como parte del plan de descentralización administrativa del MSP, se le debería entregar a cada hospital o región su respectivo presupuesto para la compra, operación y mantenimiento de equipo.

Junto con los problemas presupuestales, financieros y de fijación de precios analizados anteriormente, una de las principales fuentes de la ineficiencia del sector de la salud está constituido por problemas del mercado laboral. En relación a sus ingresos, Honduras cuenta con un número relativamente alto de médicos, pero posee uno de los índices más bajos de enfermeras profesionales del continente. El MSP se ha convertido por un gran margen, en el empleador más importante de profesionales de salud luego de aumentar en un 30 por ciento el empleo de médicos y en un 115 por ciento el empleo de enfermeras profesionales durante la Administración Reina. La capacitación de médicos y enfermeras es financiada públicamente a través de la Universidad Nacional Autónoma de Honduras (UNAH) y padece de ineficiencias múltiples y costosas. El mercado laboral se halla fuertemente influenciado por la presencia de sindicatos y asociaciones profesionales de médicos, así como por una legislación laboral compleja, incluyendo, y con particular importancia, a la *Ley del Médico Empleado*, que regula el empleo de médicos. El marco institucional ha creado rigideces que han contribuido a la concentración de médicos y enfermeras en las ciudades principales, la subutilización de hospitales y CESAMOs en las tardes, y la selección de personal inadecuado para posiciones directivas clave. Estos problemas no son problemas particulares únicamente de Honduras, y son muchos los países que luchan por reformar sus sistemas de capacitación y para introducir una mayor flexibilidad a sus mercados de trabajo. Sin duda que ésta no es una tarea fácil, y es una tarea que lleva tiempo, dado que necesita ser implementada bajo consenso. Honduras ha sido más lenta que muchos de sus vecinos para comenzar a enfrentar los problemas del mercado laboral; es tiempo de poner estos temas sobre el tapete.

En primer lugar, el Gobierno y la Universidad necesitan ponerse a trabajar juntos para producir una estrategia para la capacitación de personal del sector de la salud. Entre los aspectos principales que deben ser enfocados, se incluyen: la apertura de una rama de especialización en medicina general de familia como base para una atención de alta calidad fuera de un medio hospitalario; la implementación de medidas para reducir el elevado nivel de abandono de estudios de médicos y enfermeras profesionales; el desarrollo de programas de capacitación gerencial y el aumento de la oferta de enfermeras profesionales. En segundo término, es necesaria una reforma del sistema de pagos. En particular, dados los significativos aumentos de salario solicitados por el *Colegio Médico* durante el período previo a las elecciones, éste podría ser el momento apropiado para un debate público que establezca una relación entre los incrementos de salario y el aumento de flexibilidad necesario para mejorar la calidad y el acceso a los servicios del MSP. Algunos de los cambios que podrían ser deseables incluyen: (i) mejorar la retribución de enfermeras profesionales y demás personal auxiliar para resolver los problemas de contratación y rotación de personal de alta calidad; (ii) aumentar las bonificaciones por zonificación, de manera de resolver los problemas de contratación en zonas remotas, -- en el presente esta bonificación le corresponde solamente a los médicos, dichas retribuciones tienen un tope fijado a un nivel bajo y son pocas las áreas donde existen; (iii) establecer un vínculo entre aumentos salariales futuros y ganancias específicas en productividad, reasignación de turnos de la mañana a turnos de la tarde y noche, e indicadores de calidad (incluyendo tiempo de espera de los pacientes). Una tercer área donde la necesidad de reforma es crucial, son los criterios para el nombramiento de personal a posiciones gerenciales. El uso de nombramientos políticos debe ser abandonado, y en cambio deberá ser la capacidad gerencial el criterio primordial a utilizar en la selección de personal para esta posición.

El desarrollo de políticas para los productos farmacéuticos y la seguridad social

A principios de la década de los años noventa, se observaron mejoras significativas en materia de políticas reguladoras de productos farmacéuticos con la aprobación del Código de la Salud y una sustancial liberación del sector. Pero la gran importancia económica y médica del sector, significa que habrá de continuar requiriendo la atención prioritaria del Gobierno. Los gastos en productos farmacéuticos alcanzan casi el tres por ciento del PBI, y la mayor parte de este gasto se concreta en farmacias privadas para la automedicación. Los tres desafíos principales para los encargados de elaborar políticas en el día de hoy, son: (i) las continuadas insuficiencias de medicamentos en hospitales y centros de salud del MSP; (ii) las carencias del MSP en materia de capacidad reguladora, especialmente en el área de garantía de la calidad de los productos farmacéuticos; y (iii) la necesidad de mejorar el uso racional de medicamentos (URM).

Para mejorar la disponibilidad de medicamentos en el sector público, será necesario efectuar cambios en la cadena de suministros y en las políticas de fijación de precios. En la cadena de suministros existe la necesidad de: (i) capacitar para mejorar el manejo de inventarios; (ii) fortalecer la distribución con una combinación de inversiones selectivas y la contratación de servicios privados de transporte; (iii) continuar mejorando los procedimientos de adquisiciones abriendo a las adquisiciones públicas a la competencia internacional y adoptando una combinación menos controladora, de adquisiciones centralizadas y descentralizadas para equilibrar a las economías de escala obtenidas a través de compras centralizadas, con una mayor puntualidad y una oferta local de compras descentralizadas. Las políticas de fijación de precios para medicamentos también requieren consideración. Los medicamentos son gratis en el sector público, pero a menudo no se dispone de ellos. En las áreas urbanas, los pacientes adquieren sus medicamentos en farmacias. En las áreas rurales, cada vez es más común que los pacientes adquieran sus medicamentos en farmacias comunales (*Fondos Comunales*) que se han desarrollado rápidamente con el apoyo de ONGs y que se encuentran actualmente aprobadas por el MSP. Honduras debiera considerar duplicar la experiencia de otros países que, enfrentados con condiciones similares, reemplazando sus inoperantes farmacias públicas con fondos comunales que funcionan dentro de las clínicas públicas. Esta política podría ser suplementada por un subsidio enfocado en asegurar un abastecimiento regular de un número más limitado de medicamentos vitales seleccionados.

Las principales debilidades en materia reguladora, requieren de una respuesta técnica así como algunas reformas. El fortalecimiento de la capacidad técnica del MSP, especialmente en el área de la garantía de la calidad, requiere de capacitación, y de manera crucial, de la mejora de las retribuciones y las perspectivas profesionales del personal, de modo de poder detener la pérdida de capacidad y conocimientos en favor de un sector privado más lucrativo. En particular, son dos los problemas que requieren de una reforma: el primero, que para garantizar la objetividad, el laboratorio nacional deberá independizarse del Colegio Químico-Farmacéutico; y el segundo, que a largo plazo, podrían surgir importantes beneficios resultantes de una integración centroamericana, a través del reconocimiento mutuo de registros, a través del desarrollo de una red de control de calidad regional y a través de una agencia de autorización de comercialización común.

Finalmente, para aumentar el uso racional de medicamentos, el MSP deberá: acelerar la adopción de los "Criterios Eticos para la Promoción de Medicamentos" de la OMS; trabajar con UNAH para enfatizar el URM en el curriculum de estudios médicos y farmacológicos y trabajar con el Colegio Médico para implementar programas de capacitación en el URM para médicos.

El sistema de seguridad social hondureño (IHSS) es uno de los menos desarrollados de América Latina, cubriendo apenas al 10 por ciento de la población. La mayoría de los beneficiarios están concentrados en Tegucigalpa y San Pedro Sula, donde se encuentran situados los tres hospitales que absorben la parte del león del presupuesto del IHSS para la salud. El IHSS se encuentra atrapado en un círculo vicioso donde un rendimiento pobre ha llevado a que el sector privado se resista a incrementar el financiamiento, y la crisis presupuestal resultante se traduce en un rendimiento aún peor. La contribución efectiva a la seguridad social se hace minúscula debido a un techo de ingresos que ha estado congelado durante 30 años y que limita a apenas $3 la contribución mensual máxima al fondo de salud y maternidad por trabajador asegurado. Durante muchos años, el déficit resultante del fondo de salud ha sido financiado drenando al fondo jubilatorio administrado conjuntamente con el fondo de salud. En los últimos años, el sector privado y el Congreso se han negado a incrementar el techo de ingresos ("...hasta que desaparezca el desperdicio de los hospitales..."). La administración del IHSS ha respondido a la crisis financiera reduciendo al máximo los gastos en artículos tales como medicamentos, materiales médicos, inversión y mantenimiento, mientras que los sueldos y salarios han permanecido estables en términos reales. El resultado ha sido una crisis de rendimiento. El IHSS es menos eficiente que el MSP, en términos físicos y de costos, siendo los costos más altos debido a una sobreabundancia de personal, altos costos administrativos y baja utilización de camas.

La crisis del IHSS es tan profunda que es improbable que la institución pueda volverse eficiente sin realizar cambios estructurales. Los consultores que se han contratado para estudiar la posición financiera del IHSS y las necesidades del fondo jubilatorio, invariablemente recomiendan elevar los techos para el cálculo de contribuciones, y separar al fondo jubilatorio del fondo de salud. Estas son medidas necesarias, pero que de por sí no son suficientes, dado que dejan sin resolver a los problemas de eficiencia en la provisión de servicios de salud. La principal recomendación de este informe es que además de estas medidas, la reforma deberá concentrarse en fortalecer el papel del IHSS como asegurador público y eliminar su papel como proveedor directo de servicios. Para lograrlo, es necesario que exista una separación entre la propiedad y la administración de la red de salud, y la administración del seguro de salud. Esto podría concretarse mediante la creación de un ente autónomo separado que maneje la red de la salud; pasando los hospitales y clínicas al MSP, privatizándolos, o mediante una combinación de ambos. Esta separación es un elemento clave de la reforma propuesta, que permitiría al IHSS concentrarse en su papel como asegurador y abandonar su imagen tradicional como proveedor de servicios de la salud. Este informe se extiende en el análisis de reformas adicionales y medidas de ampliación de la capacidad que serían necesarias para otorgarle una nueva vida al IHSS. Un mensaje importante del informe es que la reforma del IHSS es necesaria no sólo para el beneficio del propio IHSS, sino que también es necesaria para evitar que se multipliquen las presiones sobre el MSP para que ofrezca servicios altamente especializados.

1. INTRODUCTION: ACHIEVEMENTS OF THE HONDURAN HEALTH SECTOR AND NEW CHALLENGES FOR THE FUTURE

ACHIEVEMENTS

Honduras may be justly proud of its achievements in health over the last three decades as the basic health indicators have improved at a fast pace (Table 1-1). During this period, the infant mortality rate has been cut by two thirds, bringing it from a level much worse than that found elsewhere in Latin America to the average level for Latin America.

Table 1-1

Improvements in health status, 1970-95				
	1970	1985	1990	1995
Life expectancy at birth, yrs.	54	64	n.a.	70
Infant mortality, per 1,000 live births /a	110	54	45	36
Percent vaccination cover BCG, children<5	n.a.	85	90	94
Global fertility rate	7.5	5.6	5.2	4.9
Percent of pregnant women attending controls	n.a.	65	73	84
Percent of population with piped water	43	n.a.	56	60
Note: Data are for the nearest available date in each case.				
/a. Direct estimates.				

To some extent, these achievements are the result of advances in Honduras' overall economic development, which has led to higher incomes, better education and more urbanization. Of particular importance has been increased access to piped water[1]. Improvements in rural sanitation through letrinization programs have also been very important: in 1993, 66% of the population had sanitary means for disposing of excreta.

However, the improvements in Honduras basic health outcomes are not solely attributable to general socio-economic development. They are due in large part to the quantity of resources Honduras has dedicated to health and more specifically to primary health programs, especially mother and child health, leading to great improvements in access and a relatively high degree of equity in resource distribution in the sector. As a result of such programs, the proportion of pregnant women who attend pre-natal clinics and the rate of vaccination coverage (BCG, DPT and measles) in children under five increased substantially (Table 1-1) placing Honduras well ahead of many of its richer neighbors in terms of access to basic services.

---

[1] Including non-piped sources, such as wells, an estimated 70% of the population had a safe water supply in 1993.

A main theme of this report is that Honduras is completing the first stage in the development of its health system and that the Government that will take office in 1998 will face the challenge of opening a second stage. The first stage consisted of the physical expansion of health care facilities and the establishment of essential elements for the provision of key basic services. The challenge for the next stage is to sustain and deepen the achievements in primary health care in what is becoming a fragile institutional environment, while responding to the growing pressure for additional clinical services from an increasingly urban and more educated population. The poor increasingly demand services such as maternity (two thirds of births in rural areas are still home-based), and better quality in the treatment for injuries and for basic surgery. The middle class demands more high-tech services and, faced with an inoperative social security system, lobbies the Government for cheap public provision of those high-end services. These new demands are compounded by the challenges that accompany population growth and urbanization and by new conditions such as AIDS.[2] The fragility of the existing arrangement arises from three features that characterize the health sector and introduce a note of caution to the overall optimism of the findings of this report. First, there is a deep divorce in the operation of the hospitals and the primary health clinics, and the improvement in the health status of the poor described in this report is based primarily on the expansion and improved operation of the clinics. Second, the primary health network is greatly dependent on donor financing and on donor-managed institutional arrangements. Third, the insufficiently examined approval of a large supplier loan for hospital equipment in 1996, and the continued pressures for the rushed approval of additional loans in the final months of the current Administration suggest the imminent risk that future public investments will repeat the mistakes of the 1970s, when the Government lost control over its investment program allowing an unplanned growth of the hospital sector (Box 1-1). Hospitals took a disproportionate weight in public expenditures during the 1980s that was only reversed in the last decade by increasing the overall fiscal effort assigned to the health sector and recurring to the then abundant external finance.

This introductory chapter details Honduras' recent achievements in resource allocation and access to health care, and goes on to identify the main new challenges for the sector. Finally, it outlines the organization of the rest of the report, which proposes a series of policy initiatives designed to meet those challenges.

FINANCIAL RESOURCES

New national health accounts, which were prepared especially for the present report on the basis of the 1995 national health expenditure survey (NHES), show that Honduras dedicates considerable resources to the sector. Per capita expenditures in health are $53, per capita public expenditures are $20.[3] Total health expenditure is estimated

---

[2] Honduras has the highest prevalence of AIDS of all countries in continental Latin America.

[3] In this report "$" means US$.

(1995) at $287 million, or 7.2% of GDP.[4]   Although the health sector is seldom discussed in economic terms, it is one of the biggest economic sectors in the Honduran economy. Total health spending in 1995 was larger than total banana exports ($214 million) or maquila production ($151 million). It was almost as large as total public investment (which averaged 8.9% of GDP in 1990-94).

Total health expenditure is higher than was suggested by previous estimates, which have tended to underplay the importance of private spending on health.[5] In fact, household expenditure on medicines and treatment (including insurance) is by far the main source of funds for health, accounting for more than half of the total (Table 1-2). Next comes government expenditure, funded out of general taxation. Funding from external agencies is

Table 1-2

Sources of finance for health sector in Honduras, 1995	$ million	Percent of total	Percent of GDP
Households' direct spending plus insurance contributions	161	56	4.1
Government (taxes)	75	26	1.9
Private firms' IHSS and insurance payments	16	5	0.4
Transfers from IHSS pension fund	3	1	0.1
External finance	33	11	0.8
Total	**287**	**100**	**7.2**

Note: Includes nutrition programs but excludes water and sanitation programs
Source: National Health Accounts - See Annex1 for details.

very large, accounting for almost a third of the expenditures of MSP providers. In recent years, most external financing has concentrated on supporting the MSP primary care network --in 1995 external sources accounted for 47% of MSP primary care expenditures (Annex 1). Social security and other insurance contributions by private firms are a small share of the total. A more detailed description of the national health accounts is given in Annex 1.

---

[4] This excludes expenditure on water and sanitation but includes nutrition programs.

[5] Previous estimates, produced by PAHO (1996) and widely cited, have suggested that total health spending is around 5% of GDP. The estimates used in this study have also made a major correction in the estimation of public expenditures by excluding the investment in water and sanitation (which amounts to almost a third of the budget of the MSP) and including the budget of several other public agencies that provide health services. Our estimates also include off-budget external support to the MSP, including external funds channeled through NGOs. See Annex 1.

ACCESS

A key factor in Honduras' good performance has been the development of the MSP network of health centers, which are the operational base for the main primary health programs. During 1990-96 the number of MSP health centers grew by 37% (Table 1-3). As a result of this expansion, MSP preventative health programs now reach the vast majority of Hondurans. The early 1990s also saw the completion of 9 area hospitals that had been under construction for more than a decade (see Table1-3). As explained in Chapters 2 and 4, these hospitals are not well integrated with the primary health clinics and consequently have not extended access in a measure proportional to their cost.

Table 1-3

MSP providers and their production, 1990-96			
	1990	1996	Growth 1990-96
Number of hospitals and health centers			
Nacional hospitals	6	6	0%
Regional hospitals	6	6	0%
Area hospitals	7	16	129%
Total, Hospitals	24	28	17%
CESAMO	177	214	21%
CESAR	516	726	41%
Centro Materno Infantil	0	10	n.a.
Total, health centers	693	950	37%
Total	**717**	**978**	**36%**
Attentions per 1,000 population			
In hospitals	323	322	-0.5%
In health centers	603	648	7.5%
Total	926	970	4.7%

Note: In 1990 Hospital Escuela was divided in the official statistics between the Maternity and Medical-Surgical blocks, while in 1996 it was treated as one hospital. In the present table, it is treated as a single institution in both years.
Source: MSP.

MSP is the main supplier of clinical health services in general, and is far and away the main provider for hospital services (Table 1-4).[6] The private sector is the second most important supplier, especially for ambulatory care.[7] In rural areas the MSP is by far the main supplier of all sorts of attention, but even there the private sector supplies a third of ambulatory consultations. In urban areas, the private sector is the main source of ambulatory attention. The IHSS is the least important supplier, with 7% of both ambulatory and preventative care and 16% of hospital care,

Table 1-4

Who attends whom: principal providers of health services (percentage)			
	Ambulatory consultation	Prevention and control	Hospital care
Total			
MSP	48	67	70
IHSS	7	7	16
Private	45	26	14
Urban			
MSP	31	52	59
IHSS	13	12	24
Private	57	35	17
Rural			
MSP	67	84	93
IHSS	0	0	0
Private	33	16	7
Source: NHES 1995.			

---

[6] Each year in Honduras, there are an estimated 8.4 million ambulatory consultations to deal with immediate health problems; 1.1 million preventative consultations and 266,000 hospitalizations.

[7] Most of this is modern medicine, commercially supplied. Traditional healers supply only 2% of ambulatory contacts and NGOs, 5%. Most NGOs concentrate their efforts on reinforcing the MSP's clinics rather than running alternative networks.

and is concentrated entirely in urban areas.

Table 1-5 shows how the choice of provider of clinical services is affected by household income. The MSP is crucial for low income households: among the poorest 20%, it supplies 68% of contacts. However, private doctors and clinics are also important, supplying 30% of services received by the poorest 20%. Among richer households, the MSP's share declines, while the private sector and IHSS increase in importance.

Table 1-5

The rich and the poor: ambulatory attentions by income quintile				
First				Fifth
(lowest)	Second	Third	Fourth	(highest)
Suppliers:	Percent who are attended by each type of supplier			
MSP	68	69	50	41	18
IHSS	2	1	8	8	12
Private	30	29	42	51	70
- Commercial	22	24	36	45	63
- NGO	8	5	5	4	5
- Traditional	2	2	2	2	2

Source: NHES 1995; based on population quintile data.

In addition to its role as a major supplier of clinical services, the private sector also has a crucial role as supplier of medicines, through the network of pharmacies and other private retailers. Private expenditure on medicines is estimated to total 37% of all health spending in Honduras (See Annex 1 for more detail on the role of different types of health expenditure).

EQUITY[8]

Although there are clear differences in access to clinical services between different income groups and between the rural and urban populations, these differences are much less marked than would be expected for a country of Honduras' unequal income distribution (Diagram 1-1). While the poorest 20% of the population receive only 3% of income, they receive 21% of preventative consultations, 17% of ambulatory clinical contacts and 15% of hospitalizations. Although wealthier households have an increased share of the total volume of use of health services, the increase is relatively small, compared with differences in income.

Health care is a good whose consumption normally rises in line with income or faster; but in Honduras, as a result of the MSP's access programs, the consumption of health services by the poor (measured in volume terms) is not much lower than that of the rich.[9] The high incidence of preventative consultations among the poorest 20% of households is a measure of the success of the MSP's rural primary care programs.

---

[8] The methodology utilized for the results described in this section is summarized in Annex 2.

[9] The data cited in the text and shown in Diagram 1-1 refer to "volume" measured by ambulatory contacts and hospital discharges.

Measured in value terms, the rich consume more health services per capita than the poor. This greater consumption by the richer household is financed privately and by the IHSS. By contrast, the rich benefit less per capita than the poor from MSP expenditures. As shown in Diagram 1-2, the MSP concentrates its resources primarily on the provision

Diagram 1-1

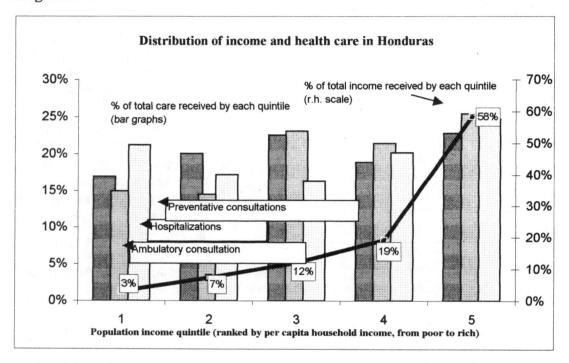

of services to households in the bottom three income quintiles, while the resources of the IHSS and private expenditures go principally to finance health care for the better off. The MSP's subsidy to health care for the poor is equivalent to 23% of the cash incomes in the bottom quintile (Diagram 1-2). The MSP is also an important agency for the redistribution of income, because the vast majority of the taxes which finance its programs are paid by the better off, while the majority of its services are consumed by the poor (Diagram A 2.1 in Annex 2).

The concentration of the expenditures of the MSP on the poor depends on several factors. First, it is the allocation of a significant share of MSP resources to primary services. Second, it is the result of the demand by the poor for MSP hospital services which has shaped many of the services provided. Poor women wanting to give birth in public hospitals have forced hospital managers to allocate more beds for this purpose. The large demand for ambulatory services by the poor have also led to an expansion of

Diagram 1-2

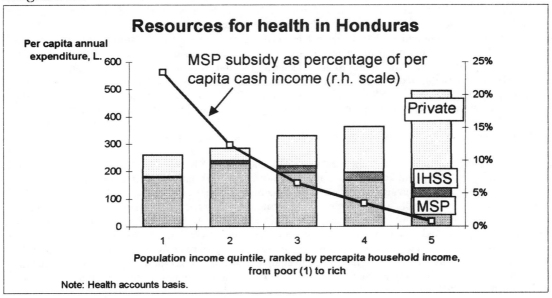

these services beyond what the hospitals saw as "their mission" of providing acute inpatient care. Third, and very importantly, it is the result of the lack of resources to purchase high-tech equipment for public hospitals that prevailed until 1996. The achievements in equity are vulnerable to future decisions on public investment, especially on high-tech hospital equipment and to the pricing of public services. This issue is extremely current, as the Government recently agreed to finance a wish list of $20 million of hospital equipment and is considering taking up two new loans, without developing a framework for any of these investments. This risks a repetition of the events of the 1970s, when the Government lost control over some of its investments and the hospital sector expanded greatly and at great cost, changing the shape of MSP and leaving behind an external health sector debt that amounted in 1997 to $292 million (see Box 1-1).

NEW CHALLENGES

Honduras has extended basic health care to the vast majority of its citizens, at the same time avoiding some of the inequitable patterns of resource distribution seen in many public health systems in developing countries. The results are patently obvious in the improving health status of its population. However, it cannot afford to rest on its laurels.

Box 1-1

Public investment running amok: lessons from the PRONASSA (Programa Nacional de Salud of the 1970s and 1980s)

In 1973, the Honduran health authorities, with the support of PAHO and USAID, developed a national health plan (PRONASSA) to extend coverage of basic services. The plan emphasized bringing simple community-based health services to the rural population and called for the construction of rural health posts and area hospitals and for the rehabilitation of two regional hospitals to replace obsolete facilities. The program was financed by a loan which was originally approved for a substantially scaled down program from what was requested by the Government. The approved loan included the construction of 8 new emergency hospitals (instead of the 10 requested), reduced the capacity of the Comayagua regional hospital from 100 to 50 beds and scaled down the size of the San Pedro Sula regional hospital from 350 beds to 245. At the time of loan approval, the final designs for the two regional hospitals (the two most expensive individual units in the program) were not completed. Perhaps more important, no consensus had been reached about the loan design and the reductions in the proposed scale of the investments were to prove illusory with the passage of time.

This project, originally planned to be completed in 4 years and to cost $16 million, changed the shape of the Ministry of Health and compromised the public investment program in health for over a decade. The project closed 4 years late, without achieving completion of the construction plan. Costs were two and a half times what was originally predicted (in real terms) causing the government's counterpart contribution to grow from an original plan of $2 million to over $17 million. At the time the project closed, only 2 area hospitals were completed (El Progreso and Puerto Cortes) and six area hospitals were left unfinished. The hospitals of Comayagua and San Pedro Sula were built expanding the scale of the former from 50 to 100 beds and of the latter from 245 to 500 beds. There was no money left to equip the hospitals. Over the years, the project forced the Government to take new loans to complete the investments. Over the longer term, it forced the Ministry to shift a massive proportion of human and financial resources to hospitals.

The original aim of strengthening basic health services was also lost in the process. The area hospitals suffered a drastic conceptual change since their formulation in the original plan to their form once the investments were completed. They were originally thought of as health centers with a strong emphasis on public health and ambulatory care that would play a significant role in supporting the delivery of basic health services by the CESARs and the community health workers. During implementation, the space for public health activities was abolished, the ambulatory care area was retained but most of the equipment, physical plant and personnel were reoriented towards inpatient care. What started off as a plan to strengthen basic health care ended up building acute care, general hospitals of fifty beds with a small ambulatory and emergency care component that is in practice divorced from the primary health system and competes with it for public resources.

Note: This box is based on the Ex-Post Evaluation carried out by the Office of the Controller of the IDB in 1987 (OER 50/87)

The achievements registered in the foregoing sections bring in their wake new risks and new challenges. Public policy should aim for a continued increase in access to care by the poor, improved quality and a more effective interaction of the private sector, the public sector and social security. It is useful to separate the new challenges facing the Government into the areas of financing, service provision and policy development and regulation. The new Government should produce a vision statement, explaining how the different sectors will interact in each of these areas. This report is designed as an input for the preparation of such a statement. The rest of this report addresses the principal challenges facing the Government in the coming years in these three areas and makes policy recommendations.

The next two chapters discuss challenges in public sector financing. Chapter 2 analyzes public sector financial management and planning procedures, while Chapter 3 analyzes the debate concerning co-payments by users of public facilities. The following two chapters discuss the main challenges in the provision of public services. Chapter 4 presents micro-economic indicators of efficiency for public clinics and hospitals and

2. MODERNIZING MSP'S FINANCIAL MANAGEMENT

Financial management in MSP is highly centralized and traditional. In the past, this had the advantage of facilitating fiscal control, while at the same time, the inefficiency costs created by centralization were not great, due to the low organizational complexity of the MSP, which managed a small number of providers with few and relatively simple tasks. However, today the system has grown and become increasingly complex. The rigidity of the old system has become an obstacle to efficient management and the budget is being circumvented by donors, making it a less effective tool for fiscal control and sectoral planning. To meet the new challenges, MSP will require a clear definition of the objectives to be pursued by its providers coupled with greater flexibility of decision making at the local level. It will also require more sophisticated information for decision making at the central level. This chapter discusses the shortcomings of MSP's existing budgetary, financial, information, administration and planning systems and presents recommendations for their reform.

THE MAIN SHORTCOMINGS

The budgetary system and resource allocation

Fragmentation of the health sector budget. Many sources of MSP financing deliberately circumvent its budget through a variety of ad-hoc arrangements. As a result,

Table 2-1

How external funders circumvent the MSP budget, 1995			
		Percent of the total which is:	
By type of agency	External funds for health, $ million	For support to MSP programs	Chanelled through MSP budget
Multilateral banks	12.0	100	36
Bilateral and U.N. Agencies	18.0	100	0
NGOs	2.5	71	0
Total	**32.5**	**98**	**13**
Source: National Health Accounts (Annex 1).			

MSP's budget is an incomplete account even of the financial flows directly relevant to MSP as service provider. A further consequence is that no one really knows what is the total of resources channeled into the public health sector, what is their regional distribution, what proportion of funds support primary health programs, where the funds come from or what activities they finance, information which is a *sine qua non* for effective sectoral planning. Data from the National Health Accounts (Annex 1) illustrate this problem well. In 1995, the total cost of MSP services was $107 million, but MSP's own budget statement captured only 64% of this total. The remainder is channeled through other government agencies, through MSP providers but out-of-budget (e.g. co-payments --see Chapter 3) or through international agency and NGO programs which support MSP as a service provider, but do not entrust its bureaucracy with the funds. For example, investment funds are channeled through FHIS or through UNDP (both of which are exempt from official procurement rules); funds for operational expenditures such as travel or gasoline are channeled through NGOs, whose role is sometimes simply to sign checks in support of MSP activities; and drugs and medical supplies are often provided in-kind by donors. External agencies by-pass MSP formal budgetary mechanisms in almost all cases (Table 2-1). In 1995, Honduras received a total $32.5 million of external finance for the health sector, of which 98% was for support to MSP programs, mainly in primary health. However, only 13% of this total ($4.2 million) was channeled through the Ministry's budget.

Use of historic budgets. The MSP budget allocates resources on the basis of past allocations, rather than reflecting a forward-looking planning process. Although the health regions make submissions to the Ministry, these are given scant consideration in the budgetary process and there is little opportunity to exercise local managerial discretion to improve the efficiency of resource allocation. In contrast, the Finance Ministry is very influential in the finalization of the budget (both the total and its composition) and directly executes most payments (including the payroll). In recent years, there has been an unsuccessful attempt to develop the budgets of health regions, linking them to desired outcomes. This attempt received insufficient technical and political support and failed to become institutionalized. The technical weaknesses included the use of unrealistic assumptions about the feasibility of service improvements in the short term, and the use of variables which are difficult to monitor or for which there was no baseline data.

An important consequence of the use of historical budgets is that the budgetary system provides no incentives for improved performance. For example, in 1991-95, the hospital budget grew by 40% in real terms, but hospital discharges grew by only 13% and outpatient visits (including emergency) by 28% with no significant changes indicating a more complex case-mix. This is not surprising, because the use of historic budgets makes it unnecessary to evaluate past performance. As a consequence, the valuable data on production of health services currently collected by the areas, the regions and the Ministry are not utilized for planning purposes.

Divorce between hospitals and the primary network. Budgeting is done separately for the hospitals and for the primary network. As a result, although in theory area and regional hospitals belong to their respective Health Regions and are subordinate to the Regional Director, in practice they remain independent. The Regional Director has little influence over the design and management of the budget approved by Congress in the name of each hospital. This divorce is reinforced by the use of political appointees for hospital directorships, which exacerbates the lack of integration of the regional networks.

Budget execution

Key problems related to budgetary execution include the following:

- **Inflexibility in reallocations**. The system outlaws the reallocation of funds budgeted for personnel, and Ministry of Finance permission is needed in many other cases to do so. Even where reallocation is formally within the discretion of MSP, the fear that it may be illegal or the knowledge that it will be administratively complex breeds immobility in the context of a bureaucratic culture which prefers to avoid risks.
- **Frozen accounts**. The Finance Ministry routinely freezes budget line items such as investment and vacant posts, for example, as part of macroeconomic spending control programs. In practice, this means that the approved budget never becomes fully available to MSP.
- **Centralized purchasing procedures**. MSP's purchasing procedures have improved following the creation in 1995 of an in-house purchasing agency (*proveeduría especial*). Nevertheless, payments still take at least two months to be completed, as they require a ministerial signature and are still executed by the national Treasury.
- **Extreme rigidity in the use of liquid funds**. The establishment of cash accounts is discouraged by the requirement that the fund administrator lodge a large personal guarantee and by unclear regulations.

Accounting, cost measurement and information systems

These are some of the MSP's weakest areas:

- There is no separate accounting system. Accounting is done simply by subtracting expenditures from the allocated budget.
- Many routine procedures, including payroll administration, are still not fully computerized. Even in areas where computer systems have been developed (e.g. in budgeting and inventory control), they are primitive. In the Health Regions and hospitals, almost all administrative systems are manual.
- There have been several attempts to develop cost measurement systems for hospitals. Unfortunately, these were abandoned before the systems became institutionalized. In most cases, these experiences also did not result in comprehensive data on the absolute or relative costs of different interventions and levels of care, or in policy actions to improve resource allocation.
- Data for decision making is routinely disorganized, usually untimely and sometimes unreliable. Although an enormous quantity of statistics is compiled within the MSP, and most of them eventually reach Tegucigalpa, the information is often neither aggregated in a way that would facilitate decision-making, nor analyzed to provide the UPSs and Health Regions with feedback on their performance. For example, the data presented below on the frequency of utilization of CESARs and on the productivity of

MSP hospitals is readily available in the MSP but is not monitored or used to inform policy decisions.

RECOMMENDATIONS

Modernizing MSP's financial management requires changes in its organizational structure and procedures. These changes must be complemented by a large investment in capacity building. The recommendations below are grouped into measures of structural reform and measures of capacity building.

Structural reform

Separating financing, provision and regulation. In the past, MSP has focused its efforts with considerable success on direct service provision, but in the future its planning and regulatory functions will assume a growing importance. Also the greater complexity of the service network requires a clear separation of the functions of financing from that of service provision. To this end, MSP should be reorganized to separate the functions of: (i) financing and sectoral planning; (ii) regulation of health services; and (iii) direct service provision. The 1997 law that reorganized some of the public administration made few changes in health. Among the changes, it created three vice-ministries. This reorganization could usefully be fine-tuned in the following way: The existing Vice-Ministry of Health Services would remain and focus its activities on the direct provision of services by MSP. A new Vice-Ministry of Financing and Administration would be charged with managing budgetary transfers to the health sector, and could also provide support to the Ministry as a whole in computation and statistics. The Vice-Ministries of Population Risks and Sectoral Policy would be joined into a single Vice-Ministry of Health Policy and Regulation.

Consolidate regionalization. While in theory MSP has been regionalized, in practice it remains highly centralized. To make regionalization real, the health regions should be constituted as autonomous public entities. Regional directors should be given responsibility for managing all establishments and programs in their region, so that area and regional hospitals would be managed jointly with the primary clinics (national hospitals would be excluded from this arrangement). The regions would be responsible for the administration of assets, the management of personnel, and the preparation and execution of the budget.

Modernize the MSP budget through payment-by-results. MSP should replace the existing historic budgets with a system of payment by results, under which autonomous health regions and national hospitals would sign management contracts with the MSP, agreeing on specific monitorable objectives within an established system of rewards and penalties.

Make MSP budget execution more flexible. Regional autonomy and payment-by-results should be complemented with greater flexibility in budget execution. The reform would give special emphasis to obtaining greater flexibility for the rules governing purchases of drugs and medical materials; the rules blocking the use of *fondos rotatorios*; and those limiting transfers between budget line items. In the medium term, the rigid rules governing personnel under the Civil Service Code should also be modernized, although this issue goes beyond the health sector.

Capacity building

Improvement of information and administration systems:

- Rationalize and document administrative procedures, with special attention to the areas of accounting, budgeting, treasury, audits, purchases, stock maintenance, payroll and hiring of personnel.
- Automatize the new administrative procedures. This process should not be limited to the central level of the Ministry, it should include at least the regional directorates and the hospitals, and the possibility of taking it down to the area directorates and into CESAMOS should be assessed.
- Coordinate efforts to develop a management information system for MSP with the ongoing effort to develop a system for the whole public sector. At present, MSP is developing a pilot for a stand-alone, partial information system (SIGAF - Sistema de Información Gerencial Administrativo-Financiera). This is risky. It should coordinate efforts to rationalize procedures and to develop information systems with the SIAF (Sistema de Información de Administración Financiera), the public-sector-wide system being developed by the MOF and the Commission for the Modernization of the State, with World Bank and IDB support.

Training of administrative staff. MSP needs to make a major investment in administrative and management skills. To this end, it should establish a "Management Development Fund", to finance training on a large scale. Previous programs tried to do this as part of wider training programs and saw their funds diverted to clinical training. To prevent this, the new fund should be geared exclusively to financing training in management and administration of health facilities.

This chapter discussed system-wide issues of MSP's financial management and made recommendations for its reform. A more specific area of concern in the financing of the health sector is that of co-payments by users of public facilities. We now turn our attention to this area.

3.   CO-PAYMENTS

Although MSP has charged its users for services during the last 20 years, the purpose of the co-payment system remains ill-defined, data on its operation are hard to come by and the official guidelines are outdated and frequently ignored. Not surprisingly, therefore, co-payments are highly controversial. Politicians and union leaders express concern about their impact on access to health services for the poor, and complain about the lack of accountability in the use of funds. This section presents data on co-payments in MSP, describes the operation of the system, discusses its shortfalls and makes recommendations for reform.

THE IMPORTANCE OF CO-PAYMENT INCOME IN THE MSP

Co-payment income covers a small proportion of MSP costs. Estimates of the income generated range from 1.5% to 3.5% of the total MSP budget (Table 3-1).[10] Nevertheless, the funds are important because they constitute liquid resources which can

Table 3-1

Co-payments income in the MSP					
	MSP data, 1996				NHES 1995
	National	Regional	Area	Total	Total
Income from co-payments	5.4	3.0	3.7	14.7	36.6
Percent of total MSP budget	2.5	3.0	3.7	1.5	3.5
Percent of MSP revenue budget minus payroll /a	4.9	11.0	10.7	4.0	10.0
Percent of users who pay	89.0	72.0	73.0	79.0	n.a.
Reported income, percent of estimated /b	37.0	63.0	109.0	54.0	n.a.
a/ The data on this row for national, regional and area hospitals are from 1995 MSP data.					
b/ Est. income is that which would result if all reported attentions generated income equal to the reported price.					

be used to solve urgent problems, free from the bureaucratic procedures described in Chapter 2. Their importance is particularly marked in regional and area hospitals, for whom access to the Tegucigalpa bureaucracy is relatively difficult, and where they are worth over 10% of the budget for non-staff recurrent expenditure (Table 3-1). It is

---

[10] The lower figure is reported by MSP and the higher figure is an estimate derived from household survey data (NHES 1995). Reasons for the discrepancy are: MSP data do not include revenues obtained by the health centers (see below); funds spent on items not permitted by the rules (such as additional staff) are not reported to the Health Regions; corruption; and estimation errors in the data survey.

notable that in national hospitals many more users are exempted from co-payments than in area hospitals.

Co-payment revenues are normally used for payments which cannot wait for processing through the normal bureaucracy. Their use for hiring staff is explicitly forbidden. Key items of expenditure funded from co-payments are food (for both patients and staff), travel expenses, and drugs and medical inputs. For health centers, the funds provide petty cash, important for day-to-day operation, and not otherwise available.

The divorce between hospitals and the primary network is reflected in the management of co-payment funds. Hospitals' funds are spent directly by the hospital administration, which must then report income and expenditures to the Health Region. In theory, hospitals should pay 10% of their income to the region, but this is not enforced. CESAMOs have less independence as they are required to deposit all income in an account controlled by the Region and part of those funds are earmarked by use for CESARs and the regional administration. Co-payments to CESARs are not contemplated by the regulations, but are universally charged. CESARs operating on the community system simply retain the funds and use them as they see fit.

Some critics of co-payments argue that they undermine access for the poor. But there is little evidence to support this. Charges are very low relative to incomes, even for the poor. The standard fee for an ambulatory consultation (including medicines) is between L.1 and L.2, and pre-natal consultation, child development clinics, family planning, control of STDs and TB are altogether exempt.[11] Prices for basic services are under 5% of what the private sector charges for the same service (Table 3-2), and they are normally waived when the patient cannot pay. Remarkably, the NHES survey, which had a nationwide sample of over 12,500 people, found few cases where sick people had been discouraged from seeking attention by MSP charges. In contrast, a parallel survey in Nicaragua, using the same methodology, found that 18% of sick people who did not seek care were deterred by cost considerations -- a finding that strengthens confidence in the methodology applied.

The real problems with co-payments are elsewhere. As presently operated, the system creates problems of equity and efficiency as it:

- provides insufficient checks on the consumption of highly subsidized tertiary hospital treatments by the non-poor;
- gives incentives to hospitals and health centers to expand production of the wrong sort of services; and
- sends irrational price signals to MSP clients about where to seek attention.

---

[11] Average per capita income for the lowest quintile of households in 1995 is estimated at L831 per year (Source: NHES survey).

Co-payments and equity. Although, the impact of co-payments on the welfare of the poor is not marked, there is another important sense in which the system does fail in its mission to promote equity. It fails to prevent wealthy users from receiving highly subsidized tertiary services. In the past this was not an important concern because few sophisticated tertiary treatments were available in MSP and the social security system was expanding and providing the service of choice for the non-poor. However, this is changing. While the social security is in decline (see below), Hospital Escuela can now perform open heart surgery, and has a renal dialysis unit, a burns unit and an intensive care unit. San Felipe Hospital has one of two radiotherapy units in Te-gucigalpa and can undertake endoscopic diagnostic tests. In each case, the charges for such services are well below their real cost and substantially below their price in the private market. For example, in San Felipe Hospital, a course of radiotherapy costs L.2,000, compared to L.20,000 in the private Emma Romero de Callejas Clinic; an endoscopic test costs L.20, compared with the private price of L.1,200.

Table 3-2

MSP hospital charges as a percent of private sector prices				
	National	Regional	Area	Total
Ambulatory consultation	2	5	4	4
Dental consultation	10	30	40	31
Laboratory tests	4	16	17	14
Thorax X Ray	9	18	29	22
Emergency consultation	2	2	3	3
5 day stay in hospital public ward including food	7	6	8	7
Normal birth	1	1	2	2
Cesarian birth	1	1	2	2
Apendicectomy	1	1	2	2
Surgical sterilization - woman	0	2	3	2
Use of operating theater	0	0	5	3
Average (unweighted)	**2**	**5**	**8**	**6**

Note: Based on simple averages of prices reported by MSP hospitals and 11 private hospitals, including 4 run by NGOs

Source: NHES survey, 1995.

As more complex and expensive interventions become increasingly available in MSP hospitals, they threaten to absorb a growing share of the budget. As in other countries, a disproportionate amount of such services will be consumed by the urban middle and upper classes. This happens because, even though the fees are highly subsidized, they still tend to be too high for the poor. Hospitals are reluctant to waive fees for such services, because they help to ration demand and because waiving the fee means a financial loss to the hospital. As a result, it is the non-poor who receive the subsidy.

Irrational incentives to service providers

The co-payment system gives hospitals and health centers a direct incentive to over-expand output of these high-cost services, because they generate cash income. Already, some 50% of co-payment income in a typical CESAMO comes from services which have high material costs, such as dentistry, laboratory tests and X-rays. The prices charged for such services are less than a third of the private sector alternatives, so it is not hard to attract clients (Table 3-2). Similarly, hospital directors interviewed for this study are beginning to think about the income raising potential of tertiary treatments. However, the cost to MSP as a whole of increasing output of such services far outstrips the resulting income. This problem of distorted incentives is created by the centralization of the expenditure budget. MSP at national level pays for the necessary inputs (sophisticated operating theater equipment, X-ray plates, laboratory reactives, advanced medicines, electricity bill, etc.) but the hospital or clinic retains the co-payment, so it has a large net income from each intervention, which is an incentive to overproduce these services.

Irrational price signals to users

The co-payment system should encourage the efficient use of the health network by giving signals about where to seek care, but at present it fails to do this. For example, MSP has a problem with non-emergency cases swamping its emergency clinics. This is hardly surprising, when the average charge for an emergency consultation is lower than that for a standard ambulatory consultation (Table 3-2). Similarly, the logic of the MSP network is that users should be encouraged to enter the system at the lowest appropriate level. However, the co-payment system conspires against this because prices in regional and area hospitals are double those of national hospitals (Table 3-2).

RECOMMENDATIONS

Co-payments play an important role in most modern systems of health financing. They give economic signals that guide the efficient use of resources, they discourage unnecessary care and they promote equity by limiting misdirected subsidies. In Honduras, the Government should re-establish the legitimacy of co-payments by making a clear statement of the system's objectives and changing its operating rules so it will meet those goals. The statement of objectives should start by making it clear that the purpose of co-payments is not to recover the full costs of producing health services. Given Honduras' level of poverty and low insurance coverage, this would be incompatible with equity of access. Instead, the system should:

- eliminate regressive subsidies to the non-poor;
- assure access by the poor through a safety net mechanism; and
- increase MSP efficiency by sending signals to users and providers, respectively, about where to seek care and what services to prioritize.

New regulations should be issued to rationalize the co-payment system, establishing:

- what services will be provided free;
- what services should receive a partial subsidy (hence requiring a co-payment);
- in what circumstances MSP should charge the full costs; and
- in what circumstances charges can be waived.

A special policy should be designed for high cost hospital interventions. The general policy should be to charge the full cost of such services. Where the patient is a beneficiary of IHSS or of private insurance, the IHSS or insurer should pay. A fund should be created to subsidize those who cannot afford to pay. As most of these interventions are elective (e.g. transplants) or chronic (e.g. renal dialysis), it would be realistic to undertake a thorough investigation of the insurance status and financial capacity of patients. If this is not done, the relative equity of Honduran health provision will be rapidly eroded as the subsidized consumption of sophisticated treatments by the non-poor absorbs an increasing share of the health resources, crowding out primary attention.

The first part of the report has dealt with issues of the financing of the health sector. We now turn to examine the efficiency of the public providers.

4. EFFICIENCY IN THE PUBLIC PROVISION OF SERVICES

As described in Chapter 1, increased access to health care has been achieved in part through a rapid expansion of the MSP network in recent years. Between 1990-96, the number of area hospitals increased by 129%, CESAMOs by 21% and CESARs by 41% (Table 4-1). However, the output of health services has lagged. In the same period, total consultations grew by 24% and consultations per inhabitant rose by 5%, which suggests that expansion has been associated with growing underutilization of facilities. This chapter presents evidence on utilization patterns, productivity and cost efficiency of the different types of provider, and makes suggestions for improvement.

PRODUCTIVITY IN THE HEALTH CENTERS

Table 4-1

Productivity in health centers			
CESAMOs: Attendance/ doctor day		CESARs: Attendance/ nurse day	
Mean 18.4 percent of CESAMOs		Mean 6.0 percent of CESARs	
5 - 9	6	< 2.5	9
10 - 14	31	2.6-4.9	29
15 - 24	25	5.0-7.4	31
25 - 34	19	7.5-9.9	17
> 35	19	10.0-12.4	7
		>12.5	8
Total	100	Total	100
Sources: CESAR data: MSP (all CESARs), CESAMO data: NHES (sample based).			

Average productivity in the primary network is low. Table 4-1 reports data on the number of consultations per doctor in CESAMOs and the number of consultations per nurse in CESARs, including preventive and curative consultations such as immunizations, pre and post natal care, growth monitoring, family planning, health education and oral rehidration.[12] In 1996, CESARs averaged just 6 consultations per nurse-day. Physicians in CESAMOs see on average under 19 patients per day.[13] There are however, important differences underlying these averages. While 38% of CESARs registered less than 5 consultations per nurse-day, 15% registered more than 10. And while 37% of CESAMOs averaged under 15 consultations per doctor-day,

---

[12] The data for CESARs is from MSP and covers all CESARs in the country. No such data is available for CESAMOs and we report for them based on a survey of about 20% of the CESAMOs in the country (the NHES survey). The sample was not designed for this specific purpose and may not be representative of all CESAMOs.

[13] CESAMOs' average labor productivity is much lower than this, at just three consultations per staff-day, reflecting both the low number of consultations per doctor and the high average ratio of support staff to doctors.

38% are above 25. However, only 19% of CESAMOs pass the benchmark of 36 consultations per doctor-day stipulated in the law regulating the conditions for the employment of physicians (LME -*Ley del Médico Empleado)*.

These low utilization levels result in high costs. According to cost analyses undertaken for the present study, when only MSP budget data is used, the unit cost of an ambulatory consultation in an MSP hospital is hardly higher than that for the ambulatory clinics, in spite of the higher qualifications and cost of the hospital staff. The higher volume of patients offsets the hospitals' higher overhead costs. Remarkably, when more precise calculations are undertaken (as in Annex 1), including off-budget support to MSP and funds channeled through the budget of other agencies in support of MSP providers, the cost of a consultation in a CESAR or CESAMO is on average 50% above that of a hospital outpatient consultation.

In some cases, low utilization results inevitably from the need to provide services in areas of low population density and difficult physical access, such as Gracias a Dios region. However, this cannot explain the low overall average, as most health centers are located in areas of relatively high population density. The main causes of health center underutilization are:

Box 4-1

Health centers in the MSP network and the Food Coupon Program

Honduras has 214 urban health centers with doctors, called CESAMOs, and 726 rural centers without doctors, called CESARs. CESAMOs vary greatly in size, but normally have one or more doctor and professional nurse, several auxiliary nurses, a laboratory, and dental surgery. Recently, as part of the effort to increase the proportion of institutional births, birthing clinics called Clínicas Materno Infantiles (CMIs) with a dozen beds have been constructed as annexes to 10 CESAMOs. The CESARs are much less complex normally with a staff of just two auxiliary nurses and a janitor. The CESAMOs serve as points of support for the CESARs in the surrounding rural communities. In contrast, coordination between health centers and area hospitals is often poor.

Clinical attention is only part of the work of the health centers. Both CESAMOs and CESARs have well defined areas of influence within which they organize networks of community volunteers and are responsible for vaccination campaigns and the annual Censo Familiar de Salud (CEFASA). CESAMOs have teams of full time promoters who work on environmental health (improving water and sewerage systems) and on the identification and eradication of vector-borne diseases (malaria, dengue, Chagas disease). Some CESARs have a promoter, too.

Recent credits, by IDA and by the IDB, have sought to strengthen the health centers through the Family Assistance Program (PRAF). This program, run by an autonomous agency and implemented by health center nurses, consists of a $4 million-per-year food coupon program, destined for pregnant and nursing mothers and children five and younger, administered through health clinics. The program was designed with the double objective of improving the nutritional status of children and attracting users to the clinics. While available information (from 1994) suggests that the coupons are well targeted to the poor, there are no reliable indications of what the impact has been on improving the nutritional status of children and on increasing utilization of the health clinics. A study will be carried out in early 1998 to ascertain the impact of the program.

- *Inappropriate locations.* Many CESAMOs are too near to hospitals which users regard as offering better services. This problem has arisen because of the divorce in the operations of hospitals and those of the primary clinics. Investments in clinics are often made neglecting the existence of hospitals. In the past, this problem was compounded by lack of coordination between MSP and FHIS (which builds the health centers) on decisions about where to locate new facilities. In practice, once a health center is built, the political pressure to staff it is impossible to resist.

- *Closures and opening hours*. When there is no nurse available, a CESAR must close. Such closures often happen, due to sickness, vacations, and training leave, and are sometimes prolonged. This problem has grown in recent years. During 1996, the average CESAR was closed for 1.03 months, compared with 0.4 months in 1993. The worst problems are on the north coast (Regions 3 and 6) and in Comayagua, where it is increasingly difficult to retain auxiliary nurses given competition from the maquila industry. The problem with CESAMOs is often their limited hours of operation and long waiting times. Health Centers are open only in the mornings, and in order to get on the list to be seen, it is often necessary to arrive before 7 am and then wait for several hours before the nurse or doctor is available.

- *Poor service quality*. The lack of demand for CESAR and CESAMO services is often caused by poor service quality. This has many aspects. In the first place, medicines are often in short supply, and in CESAMOs, laboratories are frequently closed due to staff shortages or the lack of supplies. Also, resolution capacity is low: CESARs are staffed by auxiliary nurses, most of whom have only a primary education supplemented by 10 months of nurse training. Similarly, many CESAMOs are staffed by inexperienced doctors who are completing their compulsory year of social service. Accessible alternatives therefore are more attractive.

PRODUCTIVITY IN HOSPITALS

Table 4-2 presents data for productivity in MSP hospitals. Area hospitals have the lowest productivity. Average bed occupancy rate is 60%, compared with 74% for

Table 4-2

Productivity and cost indicators for MSP hospitals, 1995						
	Total MSP	National	Regional	Area	CMI	Notes
Total patient-days occupation	1,023,308	649,162	180,125	193,347	674	1
Average length of stay	5.95	14.89	4.57	3.34	1.01	1
Average occupancy rate	70%	74%	67%	60%	15%	1
Employees / occupied bed	3.0	2.6	3.2	4.4	n.d.	2
Cost per patient - day, $						3
Total hospitalization	22.3	11.9	27.4	32.8	n.a.	
Notes: Definition: Emps/(beds*occ rate); Definition: cost per discharge / av. length of stay Source: MSP Div Hosps.						

national hospitals. The average number of employees per occupied bed is highest in area hospitals, at 4.4 compared with 2.6 in national hospitals. This results in a cost per patient-day in area hospitals three times higher than in national hospitals ($32.8 versus $11.9).

Area hospitals, however, are not homogeneous. One group, located mainly in the west of the country (San Marcos de Colón, La Esperanza, Gracias Lempira), but also including Danlí in the south-east and Puerto Cortés on the north coast, is severely underutilized, with average bed occupancy rates of 50% or less. But there is also a group of area hospitals which face high demand, with occupancy rates similar to their associated regional hospitals (Santa Barbara, Yoro, El Progreso, Tocoa, Tela).

The underutilization of area hospitals is due to a combination of user-behavior, staffing problems and inflexibility in the allocation of beds. Patients often by-pass area hospitals to go straight to regional and national hospitals. They do this partly because they believe (probably rightly) that the quality of medical attention will be better. Many area hospitals have been unable to retain specialists. When there is no specialist physician to supervise it, a hospital often simply closes a ward.

MSP hospitals of all types function at full capacity only in the mornings. Most doctors' contracts are for 7am to 1pm and they have afternoon jobs in private practice or at the university. This leads to severe waste. In the absence of specialist physicians, operating surgeries for elective surgery and the non-emergency outpatient clinics are closed. Underutilization of surgery facilities in turn lowers bed occupation rates in the corresponding wards. (Chapter 4 discusses labor market rigidities).

> ### Box 4-2
>
> #### The hospitals of the MSP
>
> There are three types of hospital: national (6), regional (6) and area (16). *National hospitals* have tertiary level capabilities in their specialized fields and on average have 400 beds. The biggest is the teaching hospital in Tegucigalpa, which has a maternity block and a general medicine block, each with some 500 beds. Other national hospitals include: San Felipe (specialized in cancer), Tórax (chest illnesses/TB), Mario Mendoza (psychiatric), Santa Rosita, and Mario Catarino Rivas, in San Pedro Sula. Apart from the latter, all the national hospitals are in Tegucigalpa.
>
> *Regional hospitals* are less sophisticated. They have 125 beds on average, and normally have specialists. There are regional hospitals in La Ceiba, Comayagua, Santa Rosa de Copán, San Pedro Sula, Choluteca and Juticalpa.
>
> The 16 *area hospitals*, located in secondary cities across the country, are the least complex. They average 56 beds and are limited to the basic specialties: pediatrics, gynecology, internal medicine, and general surgery. All regional and area hospitals have emergency rooms; of the national hospitals, only Hospital Escuela and Mario Catarino Rivas have them.

Most hospitals also have major problems with equipment supply and maintenance. Centralized decision making about equipment supply --sometimes linked to negotiations with donors-- often leads to the provision of equipment which is neither a priority for the hospital nor suitable for its needs. For example, in 1996 the director of the regional Hospital del Sur was attempting to organize a barter deal with a national hospital to exchange sophisticated but unnecessary equipment, received under a recent loan, for basic laboratory equipment and laundry machines, which he desperately needed.

Equipment is often poorly maintained and generally underutilized, partly because of the centralized organization of repairs, but also because the equipment is received as a free good by the hospital, but using and maintaining the equipment is costly. This results in an abundance of unutilized and broken equipment.

RECOMMENDATIONS

A. Health centers

- Monitor utilization. Most of the data presented in this section is already available at MSP. It should be used for a detailed diagnosis of the causes of disparate productivity, leading to recommendations on how to improve usage of the under-used centers and to assign additional resources to over-stretched centers.
- Develop regional teams to tackle the problems. During the field work for this report, many local officials voiced ideas on how to make better use of resources. Decentralization of authority would allow such ideas to be put into practice.
- Strengthen hospital/health center collaboration, starting with a pilot program for re-organizing local health services.
- Target future expansion on the remaining pockets of unattended populations. MSP should establish the demand for new health centers before authorizing construction and should resist pressures to build centers where demand is likely to be insufficient to meet minimum productivity requirements.

B. Hospitals

- Re-think the role of underutilized area hospitals. In some cases it may be appropriate to consider turning them into birthing and emergency centers and reducing the required number of specialists accordingly. This would allow the available beds to be better utilized and help increase hospital-attended births in rural areas from the present low 32%.
- Find ways to make full use of MSP hospitals in the afternoons. Although this problem is widely understood, little headway has been made to solve it. Hospital administrators believe that the doctors and unions would oppose the introduction of afternoon shifts. One possible option is to link pay increases to accepting flexibility for afternoon shifts. Another option, used in Peru, is for hospitals to hire additional doctors on contract and fund this by charges made to patients for elective surgery and outpatient consultations in the afternoon. In some cases, hospital facilities are also used to operate on private patients during the afternoons. Obviously, such mechanisms require careful oversight, to establish the rates for the rental of hospital facilities and the fees to be paid by the patients.
- As part of MSP administrative decentralization, hospitals should be given their own budgets for the purchase, operation and maintenance of equipment.

Finally, it is worth stressing that, while the above suggestions have general validity, and will be individually relevant in many MSP health centers and hospitals, it is crucial to diagnose the specific problems of each institution and locality and develop appropriate solutions. This can only happen in the framework of a more decentralized system which achieves better coordination between its diverse components at a local level. Therefore, the resolution of MSP inefficiency will be intimately related to the reform of the Ministry's budgetary and financial planning mechanisms discussed before.

As mentioned above, a source of some of the inefficiencies identified is in the area of human resources. There are problems in the supply of the necessary skills and problems in the institutions that regulate the labor market. We turn to these areas in the next chapter.

5. HUMAN RESOURCES AND THE LABOR MARKET

Together with the budgetary, financial and pricing problems discussed in Chapters 2 and 3, labor market problems are one of the main sources of inefficiency in the Honduran health system. In this section we discuss human resource development and labor market rigidities that affect the provision of health services.

HUMAN RESOURCES FOR HEALTH

In relation to its income, Honduras, is relatively well endowed with doctors, with 8.6 per 10,000 population (Table 5-1). The number of doctors is growing at 8% per year, substantially faster than total population (2.8%). On the other hand, Honduras has one of the lowest ratios of professional nurses in the continent, at 2.6 per 10,000.

Table 5-1

Latin American ratios of doctors and nurses to population		
	Physicians / 10,000	nurses / 10,000
Haiti	1.6	1.3
Bolivia	5.1	2.5
Peru	7.3	4.9
Dominican Republic	7.7	2.0
Nicaragua	8.2	5.6
Honduras	**8.6**	**2.6**
Guatemala	9.0	3.0
El Salvador	9.1	3.8
Mexico	10.7	4.0
Chile	10.8	4.2
Costa Rica	12.6	9.5
Venezuela	19.4	7.7
Argentina	26.8	5.4
Source:PAHO - Indicadores Basicos, 1996 and MSP.		

In total, Honduras has 3,300 general physicians, 1,400 specialist physicians, 1,400 professional nurses and some 10,000 qualified auxiliary nurses. MSP is by far the most important employer of medical professionals, employing a third of all qualified doctors in the country (some 1,600) and over 50% of all available nurses (5,700). During 1992-97, MSP increased its employment of physicians by 30%, of professional nurses by 115% and of auxiliary nurses by 40%. Many of the new positions had been created through temporary contracts and were regularized by the outgoing administration in 1997.

IHSS employment has remained stagnant in recent years; in 1997 it had 352 doctors, of whom 245 are specialists; 136 professional nurses; and almost 600 auxiliary nurses. IHSS is generally considered the most prestigious place for doctors to work. The UNAH (Faculty of Medicine) employs 172 doctors and 43 nurses. According to the doctors' professional body (*Colegio Médico)*, only 150 doctors are employed on labor contracts in the private sector. The number of physicians in private practice is unknown.

TRAINING AND LABOR MARKET RIGIDITIES

Training of nurses and doctors is publicly funded through the Faculty of Medicine of the National Autonomous University (UNAH). Short courses for auxiliary nurses and for environmental health workers are run by the Centro Nacional de Adiestramiento de Recursos Humanos (CENARH) of MSP, with substantial donor support. In 1990-96 Honduras graduated, on average, 237 general physicians, 36 specialists, 121 professional nurses and 234 auxiliary nurses each year.

There are many and costly inefficiencies in the training of health sector staff. The following points illustrate some of the main problems:

- The university drop out rate for doctors and professional nurses averaged 40% in 1990-96. This is partly a result of the open door policy for anyone with a secondary education, resulting in class sizes of up to 150 students, which conspires against proper learning and contributes to high drop out rates.
- The mix of medical specialists trained in Honduras reflects the teaching hospital's needs for residents, which do not necessarily correspond to the country's overall needs.
- In 1994 UNAH closed the four year bachelors' degree for professional nurses and standardized the more demanding five year *licenciatura*. This seems ill advised in view of the severe shortage of professional nurses. It has been followed by a halving in the number of students enrolled.

The labor market is heavily influenced by the presence of unions and the *Colegio Médico* (the doctors' professional body), and by complex labor legislation, including, importantly, the *Ley del Médico Empleado*. There are seven different unions in MSP, joined together in the *Coordinadora Nacional de los Trabajadores de la Salud* (CNTS). The most important individual union is SITRAMEDYS (*Sindicato de Trabajadores de Medicina y Similares*), which organizes the majority of auxiliary nurses, health promoters and technical staff in MSP. In the 1990s union-management relations in MSP have been increasingly conflictive. In the IHSS, staff belong to SITRAIHSS, and the medical staff are organized in the *Asociación de Médicos del Instituto de Seguro Social* (AMIHSS). This institutional framework has created rigidities that contribute to: (i) the concentration of doctors and nurses in major cities, (ii) the underutilization of hospitals and CESAMOs in the afternoons, and (iii) the selection of inadequate staff for key managerial positions. These issues are discussed below.

Salaries of all doctors are governed by a law (*Ley del Médico Empleado*). The *Colegio Médico* is a key player in the health sector. Its role includes oversight of the implementation of the 1985 *Ley del Médico Empleado* (LME), with provisions that include: minimum wages set by law to be paid to all doctors by public or private employers; a working day of 6 hours, during which time a general physician working in an ambulatory clinic should see 36 patients and a specialist 24; strict regulations for the payment of bonuses and criteria for the selection of staff (including managerial staff) for public posts.

In spite of the inflation of the early 1990s, there has been little or no erosion of real earnings in either MSP or IHSS. This was largely due to the enactment of a 13th and a 14th month salary in 1992 and 1995. Additionally, in early 1997, the Government increased MSP salaries by between 10% and 30%, depending on the grade level within the civil service system. In mid-1997 the Colegio Medico began lobbying Congress to reform the LME to increase Doctor wages by a factor of 5. At the time of writing this report, their proposal was to phase in that increase through annual raises of 30%-40% during 1998-2002 (the years of the future Administration).

Concentration of medical staff in major cities

MSP has problems filling both doctors' and nurses' posts outside major cities; there are also problems retaining nursing staff in the San Pedro Sula and Comayagua areas due to the abundance of alternative employment, related to maquilas. For doctors and nurses, working outside the major cities implies losing the opportunity to supplement their income with a second job. There are no offsetting benefits in either remuneration or career development terms from being away from the capital; indeed, a long absence may put an end to a doctor's chances of entering postgraduate training. For these reasons, many MSP employees who have accepted a non-metropolitan post maneuver to get their posts transferred to Tegucigalpa or another urban center, using political influence. The result is a *"fuga de plazas"* (illegal reassignments). According to an MSP staff census conducted in 1995, an astonishing 38% of personnel were no longer working in the place to which they were originally nominated.

At present a key strategy to fill rural posts is the use of trainees. Doctors and professional nurses must work a year of "social service" as a requisite to get their degree. In 1996 there were 234 doctors and 59 professional nurses in their social service year. However, these are fewer than are needed. Two thirds of the vacancies for professional nurses in their social service year remain unfilled. This is partly due to the very low remuneration ($80 a month) and partly to the declining pipeline of new graduates. Also, most doctors are assigned to urban-based CESAMOs where in practice they add to the over-supply of physicians covering the urban population, instead of serving the rural areas.

Concentration of MSP employment in the mornings leads to inefficiency

As explained in Chapter 4, most doctors' and nurses' contracts in the public sector are for morning shifts. Although the Civil Service Law and LME allow for afternoon contracts, hospitals are run by postgraduate students (residents) after 1 pm, leading to underutilization of the facilities. CESAMOs are effectively closed from 1 pm onwards.

Selection criteria for staff

LME regulates the selection of staff for public posts including hospital directors and other health sector administrators. The criteria utilized are based principally on formal medical qualifications. It is unusual for candidates to be interviewed personally, and management skills are not even considered. Under the Civil Service Code, once a person is appointed to a post, they effectively "own" it.

RECOMMENDATIONS

Many of the issues described above are not unique to Honduras, and many countries are struggling to reform their training systems and to introduce more flexibility to their labor markets. This is nowhere an easy task and it is one that takes time, as it needs to be implemented with consensus as the potential benefits of reform can easily be lost in the costs of obtaining it through pure confrontation. Having said that, many of the problems described are more serious in Honduras than in the rest of Latin America, and Honduras has been slower than many of its neighbors to begin to reform them. It is time to bring these issues into the policy agenda.

Many problems in training, especially in the production of MDs and professional nurses arise from the gap between the Government and the "autonomous" university, which has the responsibility for training but is removed from the requirements of the labor market. An institutional link needs to be developed to overcome this gap, and a training strategy needs to be developed. This strategy should keep away from the minutiae of "manpower planning" of the 1960s and 1970s, but should provide a framework guiding the different participants in training, including the donors. The economic authorities may also wish to participate, as world-wide an increasing number of doctors ranks together with high-tech investments among the key determinants for an escalation of expenditures. Essential elements that should be included in such a strategy include:

- the creation of a specialization in general family medicine as a basis for high quality attention outside a hospital environment. For years, MSP has argued unsuccessfully for the creation of this specialty;
- an analysis of the causes of the high drop out rate for doctors and professional nurses should be undertaken jointly by UNAH, MSP and donors;
- the development of specialized management skills should receive priority support. Poor management in the health sector results in part from the lack of trained health administrators. Specialized courses in management should be developed. As suggested in Chapter 2, a special fund to support the development of management skills should be created. The Masters program in public health, recently started in UNAH should also continue to receive support.
- the increase in the supply of professional nurses should become a major objective of policy. This may require *inter alia* a revision of the decision to close the bachelor course; and
- the progressive increase in the minimum curriculum and competency standards for the training of auxiliary nurses and environmental technicians to increase their problem solving capacity.

Together with training, a reform of the pay systems is needed. In particular, in view of the large salary increases being requested by the *Colegio Médico*, this might be the right time for a public debate linking pay increases with the increased flexibility needed to improve the quality and access to MSP services. Some desirable changes include:

- Improve the pay of professional nurses and other auxiliary staff. A professional nurse requires eight more years of education than an auxiliary, but earns only 57% more on average in MSP. Similarly, chronic problems with recruiting and retaining technical staff in MSP probably reflect their low relative incomes; there is little point training more laboratory technicians unless salaries are high enough to retain them.

- increase zoning payments to resolve regional staffing problems. At present only physicians can be given zoning payments, and these are capped at only 25% on top of their salary, and they only apply to Region 8 (Mosquitia) and Islas de la Bahía. Larger payments are needed, in more regions. Also, zoning payments should be available for nurses and other health sector workers. Consideration should also be given to assigning a special weight to rural experience in the evaluation of candidates for post-graduate training and study grants as is done in Chile. Programs to support the schooling of the children of rural-based professionals should also be developed.

- link future pay increases to specific gains in productivity, to reassignment from morning to afternoon and evening shifts and to quality indicators (including length of wait by patients).

A third crucial area in need of reform is the criteria for the appointment of staff to managerial positions. The use of political appointees should be abandoned, and managerial skills should become the overriding selection criteria for these position.

Until this point, the report has focused on issues directly related to the financing and provision of services by MSP. The future role of MSP, however, will need to emphasize its functions in policy development and regulation. In this respect, the next chapters go beyond the pure realm of the public sector to discuss the challenges to public policy respectively in the areas of the pharmaceutical sector and social security.

6.   THE PHARMACEUTICAL SECTOR

The early 1990s saw significant improvements in pharmaceuticals policy, with the approval of the *Código de Salud* and the liberalization of the sector. But the sector's great economic and medical importance mean that it will continue to require the Government's priority attention.   Pharmaceutical expenditures in 1995 amounted to $125 million, equivalent to 43% of total health expenditures or 3.1% of GDP. Most of this is spent in the private sector.   While MSP and IHSS combined spent $18 million, private out-of-pocket expenditures reached $107 million. Honduran households spend some 70% of their health budget on pharmaceuticals, of which an estimated 2/3 is for self-medication.

This section presents background information on recent changes in the sector and discusses three main challenges: (i) the continued drug shortage in MSP health centers and hospitals; (ii) MSP's weaknesses in regulatory and enforcement capacity especially in the area of pharmaceutical quality assurance; and (iii) the need to improve the rational use of drugs.

AN IMPROVED SECTOR: COMPETITION AND REGULATION

Most barriers to competition in the Honduran pharmaceutical sector were eliminated in the early 1990s. The 54 national manufacturers, who produce 20% of the pharmaceuticals consumed in the country, enjoy little protection. Quantitative restrictions for imports have been eliminated, and tariffs have been reduced to 1% for inputs and for final products, except for imports from Central America where there is no tariff. While a few wholesalers (*Droguerías*) retain a large share of the market, the presence of 115 wholesalers and the near elimination of the old system of exclusive representations for international companies has brought more competition. The elimination of the license-granting function of the professional pharmacist association *(Colegio Químico-Farmacéutico)* introduced fierce retail competition in urban areas, where there are today 620 pharmacies and 215 drug outlets (pharmacies licensed for a limited range of drugs). Many private doctors register as *botiquines de emergencia* from which they can retail drugs, and in rural areas, NGOs have promoted the creation of some 300 communal drug funds (*Fondos comunales*).

The 1991 *Código de Salud* and the struggle that accompanied its approval moved an important part of the responsibility for pharmaceutical regulation from the *Colegio de Farmacéuticos* to MSP. Since then, there has been progress in several areas, including a revision of the Essential Drug List and the transfer of responsibility for the registration of pharmaceutical products from the *Colegio Químico-Farmacéutico* to MSP. The public procurement of drugs has been improved with the creation of a *Proveeduría Especial* in MSP, to take over from the *Proveeduría General de la República*. In 1993 Honduras joined the technical committee for the reconciliation of differences in licensing and quality control to facilitate trade in pharmaceutical products, under the general framework of Central American integration.

The existing legislation contains the principal elements necessary for regulating the sector. Drug registration requires a quality check by the national laboratory, imported products require a certificate "along WHO lines", and the regulations contemplate random tests to monitor products after registration. Manufacturers, distributors and pharmacists are required to obtain a license and to open their premises to MSP inspectors.

PENDING ISSUES

Despite this formal apparatus and the valuable support role played by PAHO, there is concern about the regulatory and enforcement capacity of the MSP, especially in the area of quality assurance. Problems include: (i) the national laboratory is owned by the *Colegio Químico-Farmacéutico*, opening the door to questions on conflict of interest; (ii) the MSP's team of inspectors is small, inadequately trained and lacks funds to travel outside Tegucigalpa; and (iii) there is no system of pharmaco-surveillance on safety, efficacy and quality, including recall procedures.

While there are no good data on drug scarcity, there is a consensus that this is a major problem for MSP, especially for health centers. There are continued logistical problems in the centralized chain of public procurement/storage/distribution, and MSP lacks a realistic pricing policy for drugs.

The IDA-supported specialized procurement office in MSP has reduced bid-to-delivery time from 10 to 4 months and obtained better prices from suppliers, but the public supply chain continues to suffer from many shortcomings. Despite efforts to aggregate local needs to establish overall demand, most purchases are still based on historic volumes, leading to wasteful gluts and harmful shortages. Local administrators complain of long delivery delays, partly due to delays in purchases, but also to problems in the storage and distribution chain, where there has been insufficient experimentation with the use of private distributors.

To correct these problems, in 1994 MSP decentralized 20% of the drugs and medical supplies budget. But this policy, always controversial, was only partly implemented, since payment required centrally issued payment orders, leading to unused funds. In 1997, MSP reduced the decentralized amount to 6%, claiming that it had solved the problems that made decentralization necessary.

Pricing of drugs in public facilities remains controversial. Official policy is that drugs should be distributed free, but in practice drugs are often unavailable. In urban areas patients purchase drugs in the private pharmacies that usually surround the public health centers and hospitals. In rural areas, NGOs with the support of MSP, UNICEF and other agencies have promoted Communal Drug funds *(Fondos Comunales de Medicamentos)*, which sell a sub-set of the drugs in the Essential Drugs List at replacement prices. The initial capital comes from grants, and costs are contained by using volunteers to manage the fund and tax exempt NGOs to organize centralized purchases. After some initial uncertainly, in 1996 MSP officialized these funds, adopting regulations proposed by NGOs, and is now supporting them for the purchase of drugs.

Some basic steps have been taken to promote the rational use of drugs. A National Essential Drug List was introduced in the mid-1980s and the MSP is finalizing its 6th revision. The list, which now contains 260 active principles consistent with the 230 in the WHO model list, presents pharmaceuticals in generic form and divided into three categories (vital, essential and of normal use). These categories are used to implement policies and priorities. Diagnosis and treatment guidelines for the use of drugs have also been introduced in the context of priority programs such as expanded immunization, tuberculosis, diarrhea control, IRA and mother and child health. Despite this progress, there remains widespread irrational use due *inter alia* to self-medication (made easier because there is no control on the sale of prescription drugs), unregulated drug promotion and public procurement based on historic consumption (instead of epidemiology).

RECOMMENDATIONS

Specific recommendations are presented here to improve the availability of drugs in the public sector, to strengthen regulation and to enhance the rational use of drugs.

Improving drug availability in the public sector will require changes in the supply chain and in pricing. Public drug purchases should be based on epidemiological trends and local needs, not on historical purchases. There is also a need for training to improve inventory management at the local and regional level. Distribution should be strengthened with a combination of selective investments and the use of private transport services. While procurement has been simplified, there is still ample space for improvement. Important gains may accrue from opening public procurement to international competition, and Honduras should consider the introduction of a system of limited international competition, similar to the ones used in Mexico and Venezuela, where simplified procedures for pre-qualification have been developed to open the market to a larger number of bidders. The right combination of centralized and decentralized procurement needs to be found to balance the economies of scale obtained by centralized purchases with the greater timeliness and local choice of decentralized purchases.

Honduras should review its policies on the pricing of drugs and the role of *Fondos Comunales*, which are increasingly important in the provision of drugs for public sector patients in rural areas. Other countries, such as Peru, have brought the *Fondos Comunales* into the public health centers, replacing the inoperative public pharmacies. This sort of system combines community participation, improved availability of drugs, at the best possible prices, with subsidies to finance medicines for people who are unable to pay and continued free distribution of vital drugs.

The main regulatory challenges are technical and institutional. There is a need to enhance quality control by strengthening MSP's human resources and its technical and legal capacity especially in the area of quality assurance. While training is a necessary part of this, a substantial improvement of the professional prospects for the staff will be necessary to stop the drain of capacity and expertise to the private sector.

There are also two issues requiring a political commitment. First, to guarantee objectivity, the national laboratory should be made independent of the *Colegio Quimico-Farmacéutico*. Elsewhere in Central America this responsibility has been given to the ministry of health, a para-statal or an independent agency. Second, over the long run, great benefits could arise from Central American integration, by mutual recognition of registration, by developing a regional quality control network and by a common marketing authorization agency. However, these benefits are likely to materialize slowly, as integration processes are very demanding.

Finally, to enhance the rational use of drugs (RUD), MSP should collect objective information and use it for education of both health professionals and consumers. MSP has agreed to adopt WHO's "Ethical Criteria for Drug Promotion" and this should be accelerated. MSP should work with UNAH to revise the curriculum of medical and pharmacy studies to allow for greater emphasis on RUD. Also, new programs to up-date physicians on RUD guidelines should be implemented and should also be made available to the private sector.

Most of the report until now has covered areas where there has been noticeable progress in recent years. We now turn to social security, an area of policy failure.

7. SOCIAL SECURITY IN GRIDLOCK

The Honduran social security system is one of the least developed in Latin America, even when compared with the poorest countries in the region. IHSS (*Instituto Hondureño de Seguridad Social*) claims a total coverage of 1.24 million (22% of the population), of which 0.52 million are direct beneficiaries and the remainder are their qualifying dependents.[14] However, evidence from the NHES survey suggests that no more than 10% of the population is effectively covered by IHSS health insurance. Most beneficiaries are concentrated in Tegucigalpa and San Pedro Sula.

IHSS has a small network of three hospitals, 20 clinics and four emergency clinics, which provide services to the insured population and absorb the lion's share of its health budget. In 1995, IHSS' sickness, maternity and professional risk (EMRP) regime accounted for just 8% percent of total health expenditures in Honduras and 17% of all public health expenditures (Annex 1 - National Health Accounts).

A SYSTEM IN CRISIS

The EMRP program is financed by obligatory contributions totaling a nominal 7.5% of company payrolls[15]. This is already quite low by LAC standards, but the effective contribution is made minuscule due to an income ceiling of L.600 per month ($46) used for the calculation of contributions, which has been frozen for 30 years. This was originally a high ceiling, designed to allow a fair amount of progressivity in contributions, but is today lower than the minimum wage, which in mid-1997 stood at L.860. The maximum total monthly contribution per insured worker to the health and maternity fund is just $3.5.

In an effort to offset the erosion of per capita contributions by inflation, in recent years IHSS has pushed to increase the number of insured workers, reporting an 85% increase in 1990-96. However, this was more than offset by inflation, and total income fell by 10% in real terms. As a result, IHSS has been unable to match the increase in its nominal coverage with an expansion in the supply of services.

---

[14] Qualifying dependents are: children under five, and spouses for pregnancy and childbirth, only.

[15] The employer pays 5% and the employee 2.5% for the health and maternity program. In addition, they contribute, respectively, 2% and 1% for the pension fund (which covers the long term risks of *invalidez, vejez y muerte*), bringing the total contribution rate to 10.5%. The Government is supposed to contribute an additional 1% by way of subsidy, but this is not paid. There are some small regional differences.

IHSS is in a vicious circle in which poor performance has led to private sector resistance to increased funding and the resulting budgetary crisis feeds back into still worse performance.

IHSS is less efficient than MSP, in physical and in cost terms. MSP's average bed occupancy rate was 70% in 1995, compared with 57% for IHSS, and the average number of employees per occupied bed in IHSS is nearly triple that of MSP (7.9 versus 3 in 1995)[16]. Not surprisingly given these differences in physical productivity, estimates prepared for this study show that MSP hospitals are considerably more cost-efficient than those of IHSS, both for births and for other hospitalizations. The average hospitalization cost per patient day in IHSS is almost four times that of MSP (Table 7-1).[17]

Table 7-1

Comparitive cost efficiency in the IHSS and MSP, 1995		
	MSP	IHSS
Lempiras per patient discharged		
Ambulatory consultation	77	51
Emergency	86	n.a.
Births	950	1,249
General hospitalization	1,425	2,755
Total hospitalization	1,254	1,943
Cost per patient - day /a		
Total hospitalization	211	845

/a Definition: cost per discharge / av. length of stay
Sources: For MSP, these estimates are based on NHES survey data and the MSP's 1995 budget. For IHSS, they are based on IHSS budgetary and service production data for 1995.

The high cost of IHSS hospitals is not apparently related to higher levels of complexity: MSP now has similar levels of technical sophistication in its national hospitals, and a very high proportion of IHSS discharges are for normal births, which are relatively cheap. The higher costs of IHSS are due to overstaffing, high administrative costs and low utilization of beds; the latter due in part to the continuing budgetary squeeze, leading to shortages of medicines and materials.

For many years, the deficit of the EMRP regime has been partly financed by squeezing the pension fund. The two regimes are jointly administered, which facilitates such transfers. The pension rights of IHSS beneficiaries are also capped at the ceiling of L.600 per month, so that pension payments are very low, freeing resources to subsidize to the health system. Public sector employees have responded by creating their own pension funds. In the 1990s, some firms have also begun to create private (unregulated) pension funds for their employees, and to lobby to discontinue their payments to the IHSS pension fund.

---

[16] Although MSP hospitals benefit from the labor of trainee doctors and postgradute residents, this is not enough to explain why IHSS should need three times the staff-per-bed on its payroll. There is clearly heavy overstaffing in IHSS hospitals.

[17] MSP patients stay on average longer in hospital, 5.3 days compared with 2.3 for IHSS and as a consequence, MSP has a lower bed rotation (36 times a year, compared with 66). This is not a sign of relative inefficiency, but reflects a different pattern of illnesses treated, in particular, the inclusion in the MSP system of several hospitals for chronic illness (San Felipe, Tórax, Mario Mendoza), where lengths of stay are long, and the greater relative importance of childbirth in IHSS. Childbirth accounted for 54% of IHSS discharges in 1995, versus 23% in MSP.

IHSS is in a steadily tightening financial gridlock, where the conflicting interests of the system's diverse stakeholders prevent a resolution of these problems. Private sector employers and unions, who between them have a controlling position on the IHSS board, are opposed to raising the ceiling for contributions "until the system is reformed to eliminate waste". Congress has refused to approve a budget for IHSS since 1995 (a symbolic measure, since the previous budget applies by default) or to agree to new resource transfers.

For its part, the IHSS administration has not implemented structural changes. Rather, it has responded to the financial crisis by cutting to the bone discretionary expenditures on items such as drugs, medical materials, investment and maintenance. Meanwhile, wages and salaries have remained stable in real terms, reflecting the strength of the doctors' association and the employees' unions. The inevitable consequence has been an accelerating decline in service quality, leading to growing protests from doctors and users alike.

While the general climate has been one of confrontation, IHSS efforts to expand the coverage of its insured population outside the major cities have also led to the development of a new model of service provision, which might in the long run show the way forward for the system as a whole. In order to be able to collect health and maternity contributions in cities where it has no clinical facilities, IHSS has negotiated agreements with private clinics and MSP for the provision of services to IHSS beneficiaries, restricting its own role to that of financial agency and insurer. IHSS has also managed to negotiate with the employers and unions in these areas higher income ceilings of up to L.2,000 a month for the calculation of contributions. Such initiatives have been particularly important in north coast cities, where the maquila industry has expanded rapidly.

RECOMMENDATIONS

The crisis of IHSS is so deep that it is unlikely that the institution can become efficient without structural changes. The recommended reform would focus on strengthening the role of IHSS as public insurer and end its role as a direct service provider. A "Chilean option", opening the market for compulsory social insurance to competition from private insurers, was also examined, but was found unsatisfactory for Honduras. Given the weakness of IHSS, this competition would rapidly bankrupt it.

Reforming IHSS to consolidate it as a public insurance system:

- Separate the pensions fund from EMRP to prevent leakages between these funds.
- Separate the ownership and administration of the health network from the administration of the EMRP insurance. This could be done by creating a separate autonomous entity to run the health network; by passing the hospitals and clinics to MSP, by privatizing them, or by a combination of these. This separation is a key element of the proposed reform, required to allow IHSS to focus on its role as insurer and abandon its traditional focus on the supply of health services.

- Separate the health and maternity insurance from the insurance for professional risks, and create a new premium for professional risks to be paid by firms in an actuarially fair way, in proportion to the risk of the different industries, and assess the desirability of making accident insurance compulsory.
- Raise the ceilings on health and maternity contributions to a level sufficient to fund the efficient extension of all benefits under a basic insurance package to spouses, retirees and all children under 18.
- Allow beneficiaries to chose between a "closed plan" provided by selected providers with low co-payments and an "open plan" with any provider but higher co-payments.
- Allow beneficiaries to purchase *additional* coverage from private insurers.
- Reorganize IHSS into three divisions, each headed by a senior vice-president: (i) pensions, (ii) health insurance; and (iii) health services. These should be supported by an administrative and computer services division.

Recommendations for institutional strengthening include:

- The **health insurance division** should first create a new data base for health insurance,[18] which would register affiliates and control the collection of contributions. It would then progressively become involved in purchasing services, either internally of from third parties, and in developing payment mechanisms designed to promote efficiency. To this end, with support from the administrative division, it should improve its accounting, budgeting, treasury and audit systems; introduce systems for recording attentions given to individual patients; and develop cost-accounting systems.
- The **health network division** should decentralize the management of hospitals and clinics, and should progressively change its budgeting from an historical basis to a results basis, in parallel with the negotiation of arms-length service contracts with the health insurance division.

If IHSS opts for this type of reform, MSP would need to develop clear norms on the responsibility of IHSS for the provision and financing of preventive services (or more generally, of public goods). MSP should charge IHSS at full cost for services to its beneficiaries. In that context, it may also consider the creation of private wings with improved hotel services in public hospitals as a means to attract insurance beneficiaries.

---

[18] The only data base that currently exists in IHSS is designed for pension payment purposes.

ANNEX 1

Honduras' National Health Accounts

Health accounting allows us to identify the flows of funds which finance health care. These flows are first identified between the original *source of finance* and the *intermediary agents* (payers) which channel the resources into health care; and then between the intermediary agents and the *final provider*. In some cases, the original source of funds is also the intermediary agent, because they pass the funds directly to the final provider.

Health accounts for Honduras were constructed especially for the present study, on the basis of the 1995 National Health Expenditure Survey (NHES). Other sources used in the construction of these accounts include: MSP and IHSS statistics; data from the Central Bank and Ministry of Finance; data from health sector bilateral and multilateral donors and a survey of NGOs active in the health sector. A text box below details the methodology.

The main original **source of finance** for health (56% of the total in 1995) is households' expenditure on treatment and medicines, on public (IHSS) and private insurance, and on donations to NGOs. Next comes the government's budgeted expenditures funded out of general taxation (26% of the total). This is paid through the budget of the MSP, the Finance Ministry's own budget and those of the UNAH, PRAF, FHIS. Also, all government departments make payments of employers' contributions from their budgets to the IHSS. Funding from external agencies to the public sector and NGOs is 11% of the total; firms' contributions to public (IHSS) and private health insurance is 6% of the total; and the subsidy from the IHSS' retirement fund to the health program contributes the remaining 1%[19] (Table A 1.1).

The available funds are channeled to health providers through a variety of **financial agents**. A financial agent is any person or organization who gives resources directly to a provider. Some financial *sources* act as their own *agents* (e.g. a household which makes a payment directly to a private doctor or pharmacist); others channel their funds through an intermediary (e.g. a household which purchases health insurance). The financial agents involved in the Honduran health system are listed on the left hand side of Table A 1.1. Once again, by far the most important agent are private households, who

---

[19] It should be noted that the transfer of funds from the IHSS retirement program to the health program was unusually low in 1995, due to a policy of running down medicine supplies, which kept the deficit of the health and maternity program down to L.26 million (about 12% of the IHSS total health budget). In 1997, the transfer to health and maternity is likely to be much greater. Including the effects of a 25% wage award, backdated to April, expenditure is programmed at L.336 million against projected income of L239 million, a deficit of L.97 million or 29% of total expenditure.

spend 54% of the funds, more than double the funds spent by MSP (24%). It is striking that private insurers channel only 1.3% of all funds for the health sector in Honduras.

The last link in the chain of health finance are the **providers.** Table A 1.2 traces the flows between the financial agents and providers involved in the Honduran health sector. The main providers are MSP, IHSS, and private providers; the latter divided between pharmacies and providers of clinical services. The MSP provides 37% of all services (by value), the IHSS 8% and private suppliers 55%.[20] The most important private provider (by the value of production) are pharmacies, which receive 37% of all health funds; private hospitals and clinics receive 17% and NGO clinics, 1.2%.

MSP as financial agency and health service provider. Table A 1.3 gives a detailed picture of how MSP health programs were financed in 1995, showing that the MSP budget fails to reflect an important proportion of the financial flows relevant to its activities as health service provider. Of the $107 million which end up supporting MSP programs, only 64.2% are channeled directly through the Ministry of Health's budget; the rest are channeled through the Finance Ministry, the national university, PRAF, FHIS, United Nations and bilateral donor agencies, and NGOs. It is particularly striking that , in spite of the fact that the vast majority of their resources were used to support MSP primary health programs, external agencies have contrived to by-pass MSP's formal budgetary mechanisms in almost all cases (Table A 1.4). Of an estimated $32.7 million of external finance received by Honduras in 1995, the MSP was the financial agent only for 14% of the total. As a result, MSP's budget is a distorted mirror even of the financial flows directly relevant to the MSP as service provider.

Public health spending by program and in relation to GDP. MSP resources (including both budgeted and non-budgeted funds) are divided roughly evenly between the ambulatory network (46%) and hospitals (48%), with the remaining 6% used for public health programs[21] (Table A 1.3). Most of the funds channeled through non-MSP agencies were dedicated to support for the ambulatory network.

MSP programs spent 2.7% of GDP in 1995 (Table A 1.3). This is similar to previous estimates for public spending on health by agencies such as PAHO. However, it is reached in a different way. Previous estimates have included investments in water and sanitation within the definition of health spending, but have not picked up the spending in support of clinical programs channeled through off-budget mechanisms. In the present estimate, transfers for water and sanitation programs to the *Servicio Autónomo Nacional*

---

[20] The services of public agencies are not sold in the market and therefore are valued here on a budget or cost basis, while those of private providers are valued at their market price. This should be borne in mind when interpreting the relative balance between different providers, since unit costs in the public sector are considerably below the market prices of health services and medicines in the private sector. Nevertheless, data for the volume of production of health services of different sorts also underline the importance of private providers.

[21] However, as noted in Annex 2, Table A.2.1, an important proportion of hospital resources are used for ambulatory consultations, so that the proportion of the total of MSP resources for clinical attention which goes to ambulatory attention is 62%, compared with 38% for hospitalization.

de Acueductos y Alcantarillados (SANAA) have been excluded but off-budget support to the MSP's clinical programs has been included.

Box A 1.1

Sources used in the national health accounts

National Health Expenditure Survey (NHES) 1995
This survey, financed by JICA, was undertaken by Systems Science Consultants with technical assistance from Management Sciences for Health. The fieldwork was carried out by *ESA Consultores* in July and August 1995. The study had two components: a household survey with a nationwide sample of 2,500, and an institutional survey in all MSP hospitals, 20 CESAMOs, 16 CESARs, all IHSS hospitals and 11 private hospitals. The household survey sample was divided into three strata, weighted in accordance with the structure of the national population: 700 in large cities (Tegucigalpa and San Pedro Sula), 760 in small cities and 1040 in rural communities.

The household survey was the main source of information of private household expenditure on medical consultation and prescribed medicines presented in the health accounts. The survey followed a standard design for a health demand study. It registered general household characteristics, and then established the incidence of the following events: health problems in the previous fortnight; the use of preventative consultations in the previous 3 months, and seeking hospitalization in the previous 2 years. For each event registered, a detailed report was compiled, including the decision to seek care, the choice of provider, and expenditure on care and on access (including time and money). A descriptive analysis of the results of the survey methodology, frequency tables and copies of the survey forms are reported in: *SSC - The study on strategies and plans for upgrading the health status in the Republic of Honduras - Supporting Report - July 1996, pp.4-7*. For the present study, a detailed analysis of the resulting database was undertaken by ESA Consultores, to produce estimates of private health expenditure in relation to income and other socioeconomic variables.

IHSS: data are taken from the IHSS budget.

MSP: the MSP executed budget for 1995 was used as the basis for the estimates. Transfers to SANAA for water and sanitation programs were excluded. Expenditures were then grouped into: public health (inc. environmental sanitation, promotion and normative services); ambulatory network (inc. control of transmissible disease, nutrition programs and health center ambulatory attentions); and hospital network. Central administrative costs were divided pro-rata between these three groups.

Finance Ministry: the finance ministry pays the 13th and 14th month bonus of public sector employees directly from its own budget. This was estimated on the basis of the MSP salary budget.

UNAH: the university budget includes funds for the Medicine Faculty which is located in the main teaching hospital, and whose students are used as support staff there. These data are taken from the UNAH budget and treated as resources for support to the MSP's hospitals.

PRAF: the *Programa de Asignaciones Familiares* has a program of cash bonds given to women who attend maternity and child growth clinics, treated here as support to the MSP's ambulatory network. The data are from the PRAF budget.

FHIS: The Honduran Social Investment Fund undertakes all health center construction. Data on capital works for the health sector (excluding water and sanitation) are taken from the FHIS budget.

United Nations and bilateral donors: Many external resources (including from IDA) are channeled through UN agencies such as UNDP or PAHO or by bilateral donors such as USAID. Data for these resources were compiled from a survey of the agencies undertaken for the present study.

NGOs: NGOs are the preferred financial agent of many external donors, such as AID. Data on funds for health channeled through NGOs were compiled from surveys of NGOs and of donors who work with NGOs undertaken for the present study.

Private insurance: Data on private insurance were compiled from the *Comisión Nacional de Bancos y Seguros* (CNBS) and from SANITAS, a health maintenance organization not registered with the CNBS.

Medicines: Apparent consumption of medicines is estimated from Central Bank national accounts data and trade figures provided by the Ministry of Commerce and Tourism. Data on medicine purchases by the public sector are taken from MSP and IHSS budgets; data on households' purchases of doctor-prescribed medicines are estimated from the NHES; and purchases of self-prescribed medicines are calculated as a residual.

Table A 1. 1

Resources for health in Honduras: from original source to financial agent, 1995 Original sources of finance:						
Financial agents:	House-holds	Firms	Government tax income	IHSS Retire-ment fund	External	Total
Lempiras, million						
IHSS Health program	56	118	12	26		212
Ministry of Health			605		43	648
Ministry of Finance			51			51
UNAH			21			21
PRAF			8		27	34
FHIS			10		45	55
UU.NN. / Donors					82	82
ONG	3				112	115
Households	1,452					1,452
Private insurance	7	30				36
Total	**1,518**	**148**	**706**	**26**	**308**	**2,706**
Dollars, million						
IHSS Health program	5.9	12.5	1.2	2.8		22.5
Ministry of Health			64.1		4.6	68.7
Ministry of Finance			5.4			5.4
UNAH			2.2			2.2
PRAF			0.8		2.8	3.6
FHIS			1.1		4.8	5.9
UU.NN. / Donors					8.6	8.6
ONG	0.3				11.9	12.2
Households	154.0					154.0
Private insurance	0.7	3.1				3.8
Total	**160.9**	**15.7**	**74.9**	**2.8**	**32.7**	**287.0**
Percentages						
IHSS Health program	2.1	4.4	0.4	1.0		7.8
Ministry of Health			22.3		1.6	23.9
Ministry of Finance			1.9			1.9
UNAH			0.8			0.8
PRAF			0.3		1.0	1.3
FHIS			0.4		1.7	2.0
UU.NN. / Donors					3.0	3.0
ONG	0.1				4.1	4.3
Households	53.7					53.7
Private insurance	0.2	1.1				1.3
Percent of total	**56.1**	**5.5**	**26.1**	**1.0**	**11.4**	**100.0**
Percent of GDP	4.1	0.4	1.9	0.1	0.8	7.2
Memo items:						
Nominal GDP, Lempiras million	37,350					
GDP, US Dollars million	3961					
Exchange rate	Lempiras 9.43 = $ 1					
Source: see text						

Table A 1. 2

| | **Resources for health in Honduras: from financial agents to service providers, 1995** | | | | | | | | | | |
| | **Financial agents** | | | | | | | | | | |
Providers	IHSS	Ministry of Health	Ministry of Finance	UNAH	PRAF	FHIS	NNUU/donors	ONG	House-holds	Private insurance	Total
	Lempiras, million										
IHSS	209										**209**
Ministry of health	1	648	51	21	34	55	82	82	37		**1,010**
Private hosp. and clinics	2								409	36	**448**
ONGs								33			**33**
Pharmacies									1,006		**1,006**
Total	**212**	**648**	**51**	**21**	**34**	**55**	**82**	**115**	**1,452**	**36**	**2,706**
	Dollars, million										
IHSS	22.1										**22.1**
Ministry of health	0.1	68.7	5.4	2.2	3.6	5.9	8.6	8.7	3.9	0.0	**107.1**
Private hosp. and clinics	0.3								43.4	3.8	**47.5**
ONGs								3.5			**3.5**
Pharmacies									106.7		**106.7**
Total	**22.5**	**68.7**	**5.4**	**2.2**	**3.6**	**5.9**	**8.6**	**12.2**	**154.0**	**3.8**	**287.0**
	Percentages										
IHSS	7.7										**7.7**
Ministry of health		23.9	1.9	0.8	1.3	2.0	3.0	3.0	1.4	0.0	**37.3**
Private hospitals and clinics	0.1								15.1	1.3	**16.5**
ONGs								1.2			**1.2**
Pharmacies									37.2		**37.2**
Percent of total	**7.8**	**23.9**	**1.9**	**0.8**	**1.3**	**2.0**	**3.0**	**4.3**	**53.7**	**1.3**	**100.0**
Percent of GDP	0.6	1.7	0.1	0.1	0.1	0.1	0.2	0.3	3.9	0.1	7.2
Memo items:											
Nominal GDP, Lempiras million	37350										
Exchange rate	9.43										
Source: see text											

Table A 1. 3

Financing of MSP expenditures program, 1995										
				Financing agents						
Providers	IHSS	Ministry of health	Ministry of finance	UNAH	PRAF	FHIS	NNUU / donors	ONG	House-holds	Total
Lempiras, million										
MSP-public health		59	5							63
MSP-hospitals	1	413	28	21					22	485
MSP-ambulatory network		176	18		34	55	82	82	14	462
Total	**1**	**648**	**51**	**21**	**34**	**55**	**82**	**82**	**37**	**1,010**
Dollars, million										
MSP-public health		6.2	0.5							6.7
MSP-hospitals	0.1	43.8	2.9	2.2					2.3	51.4
MSP-ambulatory network		18.7	1.9		3.6	5.9	8.6	8.7	1.5	48.9
Total	**0.1**	**68.7**	**5.4**	**2.2**	**3.6**	**5.9**	**8.6**	**8.7**	**3.9**	**107.1**
Percentages										
MSP-public health		5.8	0.5							6.3
MSP-hospitals		40.9	2.7	2.1					2.2	48.0
MSP-ambulatory network		17.4	1.8		3.4	5.5	8.1	8.1	1.4	45.7
Percent of total	**0.0**	**64.2**	**5.0**	**2.1**	**3.4**	**5.5**	**8.1**	**8.1**	**3.6**	**100.0**
Percent of GDP	**0.00**	**1.74**	**0.14**	**0.06**	**0.09**	**0.15**	**0.22**	**0.22**	**0.10**	**2.70**

Memo item:
Nominal GDP, Lempiras million   37350
Exchange rate   9.43
Source: see text

Table A 1. 4

External funds for health and the financial agents which channel them, 1995

Financial agents in Honduras:	External sources of finance:			
	Multilateral banks	Bilateral and U.N. agencies	NGOs	Total
Lempiras, million				
MSP	41	2		**43.3**
PRAF	5	22		**26**
FHIS	30	15		**45**
NNUU / donor	37	45		**82**
ONGs		88	24	**112**
Total	**113**	**171**	**24**	**308**
US Dollars, million				
MSP	4.4	0.2		4.6
PRAF	0.5	2.3		2.8
FHIS	3.2	1.6		4.8
U.N. or donor	3.9	4.7		8.6
ONGS		9.3	2.5	11.9
Total	**12.0**	**18.2**	**2.5**	**32.7**
Percentages				
MSP	13.4	0.6		**14.0**
PRAF	1.5	7.0		**8.6**
FHIS	9.8	4.8		**14.6**
NNUU / donor	12.0	14.5		**26.5**
ONGS		28.6	7.7	**36.3**
Percentage of total	36.7	55.6	7.7	100.0
Percentage of GDP	**0.30**	**0.46**	**0.06**	**0.83**

Memo items:

Nominal GDP, Lempiras million	37350
Exchange rate	9.43
Source: see text	

ANNEX 2

Methodology of the equity analysis

This annex describes the methodology and documents the sources used in the present study for the analysis of public health expenditures across income groups. It includes a description of the methodology used to estimate unit costs in MSP and IHSS. It also explains the assumptions used to estimate the distribution of the tax burden across income groups.

The incidence of use of MSP services. The estimate of the incidence of use of MSP services is based on the results of the National Health Expenditure Survey of 1995 (NHES 1995). The household income data are also taken from the NHES. The cost of production data for MSP services are based on the NHES (institutional component), on budget data for the MSP and other public institutions and on the national health accounts for external resources. The following paragraphs detail the steps taken in the analysis.

The NHES household module collected data on both the number of different sorts of health consultations received by a household and on the household's income. This provides a basis for estimating Table 1.5 in the main text, which shows what provider caters for each income group.

There are two ways to analyze who benefits from the services provided by MSP and IHSS. (i) Estimating the share of each type of consultation consumed by each income group (distribution of volume produced). This was done using NHES and is reported in Table A 2. 1a. Income groups are defined as population quintiles grouped by per capita household income. (ii) Estimating the distribution of the expenditures (distribution of value produced). This is based on the previous step and on an estimate of the cost of each type of consultation. The estimation of the unit costs of each type of consultation is explained below.

No data is available on unit costs from MSP. The only financial information readily available is budgetary allocations to the different levels of attention (Hospitals and ambulatory network). For CESARs and CESAMOs, where the service provided is relatively homogenous (ambulatory consultations), unit costs were estimated by dividing total financial resources assigned (including capital expenditures, a proportionate share of the Ministry's administrative costs and resources channeled by NGOs and bilateral agencies and other Government agencies such as FHIS and PRAF in support of MSP providers) by the number of attentions registered. This results in an estimate of L.144 per attention in the ambulatory network (Table A 2. 1). It is noteworthy that if this estimate was made using only the MSP budget, it would be halved to L.73.

For hospitals, the analysis of costs is more complex, as hospitals provide both ambulatory consultations and hospitalizations of differing complexity and cost. Nevertheless, using data gathered in the institutional module of the NHES, it was possible to make an estimate of the relative costs of different hospital-based services, which was then used together with service production data to distribute the total hospital budget between different types of attention and estimate the absolute unit cost of each group of services. Hospital contacts were grouped into three parts: ambulatory consultations (inc. emergency)[22]; hospitalization for births; and other hospitalizations. Using the NHES institutional module data on staff numbers and costs in different departments of the MSP hospitals, an estimate was made of the total labor cost for each group of attentions. On the basis of this estimate, a relative unit cost was calculated for the three types of attention, by dividing total labor cost by the number of each type of attentions registered in MSP statistics for 1995. The total MSP hospital budget for 1995 (once again, including both administrative costs and capital expenditures) was then used to estimate the total unit cost of each type of hospital contact. The results are reported in Table A 2. 1b.

The next step in the analysis was to estimate total MSP expenditure on each income decile by applying the unit cost of each type of attention to the estimated number of attentions received (Table A 2. 1c and Diagram 1.1 in the main text).[23]

An important qualification to the analysis reported here is that the NHES data do not permit a distinction between hospitalizations of differing cost and complexity, apart from separating maternity from the rest. As explained in the main report, the more complex and costly hospitalizations are likely to be consumed disproportionately by wealthier people. At present, the proportion of total MSP hospital resources dedicated to such interventions is still relatively small, so the result of the analysis is not likely to be greatly affected. However, in coming years with the new investments underway in high-tech hospital equipment, this proportion is likely to grow sharply, making it important carefully to monitor the distribution of such attentions in the future.

Estimate of the tax burden by household income decile. Progressivity of health expenditure can also be analyzed by looking not only who gets the resources, but also who pays for them. The final source of finance for subsidized public expenditure on health is general taxation. The distribution of the tax burden by household income decile was estimated on the basis of fiscal statistics and household income data from the NHES, in

---

[22] Initially separate estimates were made for emergency and non-emergency consultations but these were found to be very similar, so they were grouped together to simplify the analysis. The similarity in the cost of emergency and non emergency consultation is an indicator of the degree of abuse of emergency clinics for routine consultations (see the chapter on efficiency of the MSP network for a discussion of this point).

[23] It was not necessary to make a correction to take account of user payments as these are not included in the MSP budget and are re-spent by the institution which receives them. Therefore, the total subsidy in the system is equal to the budget plus the non-budgeted transfers channeled through MSP providers (explained in Annex 1). There is an implicit assumption that there are no important elements of cross-subsidy based on differential user payments between different services within the same institution. However, since total user payments are no more than 3.5% of the total MSP budget, any cross subsidy based on these resources is unlikely to be important.

the following way. First, tax income was divided into indirect taxes (70% of all tax income) and direct taxes (30%). Indirect taxes were assumed to be distributed in direct proportion to income.[24]

Next, a detailed analysis was undertaken of the NHES database to identify all sources of personal income which would be affected by income tax (those in the formal sector with earnings above the tax-free threshold which obtained in 1995) and to calculate the apparent income tax contribution on each of these incomes. The result of this exercise suggested that 80% of all income taxes are paid by households in the top 10% of household income; 14% by households in the second highest decile; 4% in the third highest and 2% in the forth highest decile.[25] In the remaining deciles all reported incomes lay either below the tax threshold or were in informal sector activities which would not be caught in the tax net. It is worth emphasizing that this pattern of tax distribution is the result, not of a highly progressive tax system, but rather of a highly skewed income distribution coupled with a relatively neutral tax system.

On the basis of the preceding analysis, a tax concentration curve was constructed, showing the cumulative proportion of total taxes contributed by households, ordered by percapita income, from lowest to highest. The lowest income decile contributes 1% of all taxes; the bottom 50% contribute 11%; and the top decile contributes 54% of all tax income, according to the results of our analysis.

On the same graph, a health subsidy concentration curve was plotted, showing the cumulative proportion of MSP subsidy received by households, once again ordered by percapita income. This curve shows that (as was tabulated in Table A 2. 1) the lowest income decile receives 9% of the total subsidy; the bottom 50% receive 57% of the total; and the highest decile receive only 5%.

The area between the two curves is an indicator of the redistribution of resources from better off to worse off households through the medium of the MSP. If the two curves were coincident, there would be no redistribution; and if the tax curve lay above the subsidy curve over all the range, the system as a whole would be regressive (transferring resources from the poor to the rich). If the two curves crossed the progressivity of the system would be ambiguous.

---

[24] This simplifying assumption is justified by the following considerations. First, it is likely that the saving rate is higher in the richer deciles, thus reducing *ceteris paribus* their ratio of indirect taxes to income. But on the other hand, Honduras has a series of indirect taxes targeted on luxury consumption, such as vehicles, and the proportion of the expenditure on low income households which is spent in the informal sector, avoiding sales taxes, is likely to be higher than that for the better-off. It was assumed that these factors offset one another and the distribution of indirect taxes is proportional with income.

[25] Around half of Honduran income tax is corporate, paid on profits prior to the distribution of dividends, while half is levied on personal incomes. In 1995, the rate structure for corporate income tax was the same as that for personal income tax, except that there was no tax-free band. Implicitly, the analysis supposed that the incidence of corporate income taxes at a household level is at least as skewed as that of personal income taxes. In fact, it is likely to be even more skewed, because shareholding in formal sector enterprises is concentrated in the top decile.

Diagram A.2- 1

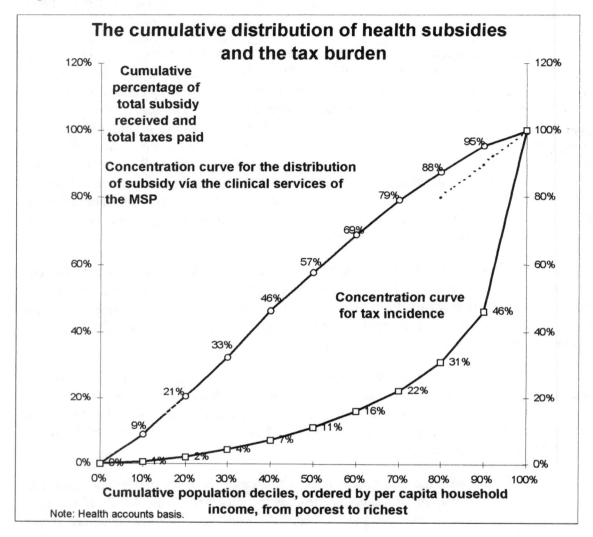

To quantify the amount of redistribution, a "redistribution index" was defined. The index number, R, is given by the sum: area under the subsidy curve less the area under the tax curve in the Diagram A.2-1. Defined in this way, R is positive when there is redistribution from the richer households to the poorer households; it takes the value zero when the curves coincide; and is negative when there is redistribution from poorer to richer households. In the case of Honduras, the area under the subsidy curve is 0.55 (55% of the area of the whole rectangle); the area under the tax curve is 0.19 and the value of R = 0.35. Therefore, we can conclude that the MSP is a highly redistributive agency.

Resources assigned to health care by all sorts of provider. The analysis of the distribution of MSP resources and of private health expenditures by income decile, described in the foregoing sections, was complemented by a similar analysis of IHSS expenditure by household income decile.

The same procedures were used as for the MSP estimates, except that the estimate of the unit cost of different types of attention was based on IHSS budgetary and service production data, rather than using NHES data. The budget and production data for each IHSS hospital and clinic were analyzed, yielding an estimated unit cost for 1995 of L.47 per ambulatory consultation and L.1,943 per hospitalization. Together with the NHES data for the number of IHSS attentions of each sort received by each income decile, this allowed the calculation of total IHSS resources dedicated to each income decile. The data for each type of expenditure (MSP, IHSS, private) were then regrouped into income quintiles and graphed to show the contribution of each to total health resources received by each quintile.[26]

---

[26] The sample size was not large enough to produce reliable estimates at decile level for the IHSS, given the relatively low incidence of IHSS attentions.

Table A 2. 1

Estimate of total MSP expenditure by income decile					
		Ambulatory consultation and emergency		Hospitalization	
Decile	Total attentions	Cesar/Cesamo	Hospital	Maternity	Other cause
Distribution of MSP attentions (NHES data)					
Total	100%	100%	100%	100%	100%
1	9%	10%	8%	8%	9%
2	13%	12%	16%	8%	9%
3	13%	16%	9%	6%	7%
4	14%	17%	10%	7%	12%
5	12%	12%	13%	11%	9%
6	10%	10%	9%	14%	15%
7	12%	10%	17%	16%	5%
8	7%	6%	8%	13%	14%
9	7%	5%	8%	11%	11%
10	3%	2%	3%	7%	10%
Estimate of unit costs					
Number of attentions (MSP data)	5,548,728	3,214,828	2,139,300	69,800	124,800
Relative cost of attentions		1.5	1	12	18
Cost per attention, Lempiras		144	93	1114	1671
Total expenditure	947,000,000	462,000,000	198,640,802	77,773,821	208,585,377

Distribution of expenditure						
		Ambulatory consultation and emergency			Hospitalization	
Decile	Total	Cesar/Cesamo	Hospital	Total	Maternity	Other cause
Total	100%	49%	21%	70%	8%	22%
1	8.9%	4.7%	1.7%	6.3%	0.7%	1.9%
2	11.7%	5.7%	3.4%	9.1%	0.7%	1.9%
3	12.0%	8.0%	1.9%	9.9%	0.5%	1.5%
4	13.8%	8.4%	2.1%	10.5%	0.6%	2.7%
5	11.1%	5.7%	2.7%	8.4%	0.9%	1.9%
6	11.3%	5.0%	1.8%	6.8%	1.1%	3.4%
7	10.4%	4.6%	3.5%	8.1%	1.3%	1.0%
8	8.6%	2.8%	1.7%	4.5%	1.1%	3.0%
9	7.6%	2.6%	1.7%	4.2%	0.9%	2.5%
10	4.3%	1.0%	0.6%	1.7%	0.5%	2.1%

Table A 2. 2

Per capita private health expenditure as a proportion of per capita income (percent)										
Decile										
	1	2	3	4	5	6	7	8	9	10	Average
Ambulatory consultation											
Total	9.6	3.7	2.6	1.5	2.7	2.6	2.1	2.0	1.8	1.3	1.5
Urban	6.6	3.2	7.4	3.4	1.8	3.3	2.4	2.0	1.7	0.8	1.8
Rural	10.3	1.9	1.5	1.3	1.8	2.3	1.5	0.9	0.6	0.3	1.1
Hospitalization											
Total	1.0	0.4	0.5	3.0	0.1	0.2	0.5	0.4	0.9	0.2	1.0
Urban	0.8	0.4	0.4	11.0	0.3	0.5	0.9	0.6	1.5	0.3	0.9
Rural	0.7	0.4	0.5	0.1	0.0	0.1	0.2	0.2	0.0	0.1	0.5
Prevention and control											
Total	1.4	0.1	0.1	0.3	0.3	0.4	0.5	0.3	0.5	0.2	0.3
Urban	5.8	0.1	0.2	0.6	0.5	0.5	0.5	0.4	0.5	0.2	0.3
Rural	0.8	0.1	0.1	0.2	0.2	0.0	0.5	0.2	0.2	0.1	0.1
Total expenditure											
Total	12.0	4.2	3.3	4.7	3.1	3.2	3.1	2.7	3.1	1.7	2.8
Urban	13.2	3.8	7.9	15.1	2.6	4.3	3.8	3.1	3.7	1.3	3.1
Rural	11.8	2.3	2.1	1.5	2.0	2.5	2.2	1.3	0.8	0.4	1.7

Table A 2. 3

How co-payment changes vary by income quintile (population quintiles)						
	Percent of users who were charged.			Average charge levied on those who paid, Lempiras		
Quintile	Ambulatory consultation	Prevention/ control	Hospitalization	Ambulatory consultation	Prevention/ control.	Hospitalization
1 (low)	88	51	81	5.4	6.1	41.0
2	94	62	72	3.4	2.9	62.8
3	92	62	74	3.2	9.6	85.8
4	90	59	84	9.0	6.4	71.6
5 (high)	92	45	77	3.2	12.6	116.4
total	91	56	78	4.8	7.0	76.6
Source:NHES 1995.						

Distributors of World Bank Publications

Prices and credit terms vary from country to country. Consult your local distributor before placing an order.

ARGENTINA
Oficina del Libro Internacional
Av. Cordoba 1877
1120 Buenos Aires
Tel: (54 11) 815-8354
Fax: (54 11) 815-8156
E-mail: olilibro@satlink.com

AUSTRALIA, FIJI, PAPUA NEW GUINEA, SOLOMON ISLANDS, VANUATU, AND WESTERN SAMOA
D.A. Information Services
648 Whitehorse Road
Mitcham 3132
Victoria
Tel: (61) 3 9210 7777
Fax: (61) 3 9210 7788
E-mail: service@dadirect.com.au
URL: http://www.dadirect.com.au

AUSTRIA
Gerold and Co.
Weihburggasse 26
A-1011 Wien
Tel: (43 1) 512-47-31-0
Fax: (43 1) 512-47-31-29
URL: http://www.gerold.co/at.online

BANGLADESH
Micro Industries Development
Assistance Society (MIDAS)
House 5, Road 16
Dhanmondi R/Area
Dhaka 1209
Tel: (880 2) 326427
Fax: (880 2) 811188

BELGIUM
Jean De Lannoy
Av. du Roi 202
1060 Brussels
Tel: (32 2) 538-5169
Fax: (32 2) 538-0841

BRAZIL
Publicações Tecnicas Internacionais Ltda.
Rua Peixoto Gomide, 209
01409 Sao Paulo, SP.
Tel: (55 11) 259-6644
Fax: (55 11) 258-6990
E-mail: postmaster@pti.uol.br
URL: http://www.uol.br

CANADA
Renouf Publishing Co. Ltd.
5369 Canotek Road
Ottawa, Ontario K1J 9J3
Tel: (613) 745-2665
Fax: (613) 745-7660
E-mail: order.dept@renoufbooks.com
URL: http://www.renoufbooks.com

CHINA
China Financial & Economic
Publishing House
8, Da Fo Si Dong Jie
Beijing
Tel: (86 10) 6333-8257
Fax: (86 10) 6401-7365
China Book Import Centre
P.O. Box 2825
Beijing

COLOMBIA
Infoenlace Ltda.
Carrera 6 No. 51-21
Apartado Aereo 34270
Santafé de Bogotá, D.C.
Tel: (57 1) 285-2798
Fax: (57 1) 285-2798

COTE D'IVOIRE
Center d'Edition et de Diffusion Africaines
(CEDA)
04 B.P. 541
Abidjan 04
Tel: (225) 24 6510/24 6511
Fax: (225) 25 0567

CYPRUS
Center for Applied Research
Cyprus College
6, Diogenes Street, Engomi
P.O. Box 2006
Nicosia
Tel: (357 2) 44-1730
Fax: (357 2) 46-2051

CZECH REPUBLIC
National Information Center
prodejna, Konviktska 5
CS – 113 57 Prague 1
Tel: (42 2) 2422-9433
Fax: (42 2) 2422-1484
URL: http://www.nis.cz/

DENMARK
SamfundsLitteratur
Rosenoerns Allé 11
DK-1970 Frederiksberg C
Tel: (45 31) 351942
Fax: (45 31) 357822
URL: http://www.sl.cbs.dk

ECUADOR
Libri Mundi
Libreria Internacional
P.O. Box 17-01-3029
Juan Leon Mera 851
Quito
Tel: (593 2) 521-606; (593 2) 544-185
Fax: (593 2) 504-209
E-mail: librimu1@librimundi.com.ec
E-mail: librimu2@librimundi.com.ec

EGYPT, ARAB REPUBLIC OF
Al Ahram Distribution Agency
Al Galaa Street
Cairo
Tel: (20 2) 578-6083
Fax: (20 2) 578-6833
The Middle East Observer
41, Sherif Street
Cairo
Tel: (20 2) 393-9732
Fax: (20 2) 393-9732

FINLAND
Akateeminen Kirjakauppa
P.O. Box 128
FIN-00101 Helsinki
Tel: (358 0) 121 4418
Fax: (358 0) 121 4435
E-mail: akatilaus@stockmann.fi
URL: http://www.akateeminen.com/

FRANCE
World Bank Publications
66, avenue d'Iéna
75116 Paris
Tel: (33 1) 40-69-30-56/57
Fax: (33 1) 40-69-30-68

GERMANY
UNO-Verlag
Poppelsdorfer Allee 55
53115 Bonn
Tel: (49 228) 949020
Fax: (49 228) 217492
URL: http://www.uno-verlag.de
E-mail: unoverlag@aol.com

GHANA
Epp Books Services
P.O. Box 44
TUC
Accra

GREECE
Papasotiriou S.A.
35, Stournara Str.
106 82 Athens
Tel: (30 1) 364-1826
Fax: (30 1) 364-8254

HAITI
Culture Diffusion
5, Rue Capois
C.P. 257
Port-au-Prince
Tel: (509) 23 9260
Fax: (509) 23 4858

HONG KONG, MACAO
Asia 2000 Ltd.
Sales & Circulation Department
Seabird House, unit 1101-02
22-28 Wyndham Street, Central
Hong Kong
Tel: (852) 2530-1409
Fax: (852) 2526-1107
E-mail: sales@asia2000.com.hk
URL: http://www.asia2000.com.hk

HUNGARY
Euro Info Service
Margitszgeti Europa Haz
H-1138 Budapest
Tel: (36 1) 350 80 24, 350 80 25
Fax: (36 1) 350 90 32
E-mail: euroinfo@mail.matav.hu

INDIA
Allied Publishers Ltd.
751 Mount Road
Madras - 600 002
Tel: (91 44) 852-3938
Fax: (91 44) 852-0649

INDONESIA
Pt. Indira Limited
Jalan Borobudur 20
P.O. Box 181
Jakarta 10320
Tel: (62 21) 390-4290
Fax: (62 21) 390-4289

IRAN
Ketab Sara Co. Publishers
Khaled Eslamboli Ave., 6th Street
Delafrooz Alley No. 8
P.O. Box 15745-733
Tehran 15117
Tel: (98 21) 8717819; 8716104
Fax: (98 21) 8712479
E-mail: ketab-sara@neda.net.ir
Kowkab Publishers
P.O. Box 19575-511
Tehran
Tel: (98 21) 258-3723
Fax: (98 21) 258-3723

IRELAND
Government Supplies Agency
Oifig an tSoláthair
4-5 Harcourt Road
Dublin 2
Tel: (353 1) 661-3111
Fax: (353 1) 475-2670

ISRAEL
Yozmot Literature Ltd.
P.O. Box 56055
3 Yohanan Hasandar Street
Tel Aviv 61560
Tel: (972 3) 5285-397
Fax: (972 3) 5285-397
R.O.Y. International
PO Box 13056
Tel Aviv 61130
Tel: (972 3) 5461423
Fax: (972 3) 5461442
E-mail: royil@netvision.net.il
Palestinian Authority/Middle East
Index Information Services
P.O.B. 19502 Jerusalem
Tel: (972 2) 6271219
Fax: (972 2) 6271634

ITALY
Licosa Commissionaria Sansoni SPA
Via Duca Di Calabria, 1/1
Casella Postale 552
50125 Firenze
Tel: (55) 645-415
Fax: (55) 641-257
E-mail: licosa@ftbcc.it
URL: http://www.ftbcc.it/licosa

JAMAICA
Ian Randle Publishers Ltd.
206 Old Hope Road, Kingston 6
Tel: 876-927-2085
Fax: 876-977-0243
E-mail: irpl@colis.com

JAPAN
Eastern Book Service
3-13 Hongo 3-chome, Bunkyo-ku
Tokyo 113
Tel: (81 3) 3818-0861
Fax: (81 3) 3818-0864
E-mail: orders@svt-ebs.co.jp
URL: http://www.bekkoame.or.jp/~svt-ebs

KENYA
Africa Book Service (E.A.) Ltd.
Quaran House, Mfangano Street
P.O. Box 45245
Nairobi
Tel: (254 2) 223 641
Fax: (254 2) 330 272

KOREA, REPUBLIC OF
Daejon Trading Co. Ltd.
P.O. Box 34, Youida, 706 Seoun Bldg
44-6 Youido-Dong, Yeongchengpo-Ku
Seoul
Tel: (82 2) 785-1631/4
Fax: (82 2) 784-0315

MALAYSIA
University of Malaya Cooperative
Bookshop, Limited
P.O. Box 1127
Jalan Pantai Baru
59700 Kuala Lumpur
Tel: (60 3) 756-5000
Fax: (60 3) 755-4424
E-mail: umkoop@tm.net.my

MEXICO
INFOTEC
Av. San Fernando No. 37
Col. Toriello Guerra
14050 Mexico, D.F.
Tel: (52 5) 624-2800
Fax: (52 5) 624-2822
E-mail: infotec@rtn.net.mx
URL: http://rtn.net.mx
Mundi-Prensa Mexico S.A. de C.V.
c/Rio Panuco, 141-Colonia Cuauhtemoc
06500 Mexico, D.F.
Tel: (52 5) 533-5658
Fax: (52 5) 514-6799

NEPAL
Everest Media International Services (P) Ltd.
GPO Box 5443
Kathmandu
Tel: (977 1) 472 152
Fax: (977 1) 224 431

NETHERLANDS
De Lindeboom/InOr-Publikaties
P.O. Box 202, 7480 AE Haaksbergen
Tel: (31 53) 574-0004
Fax: (31 53) 572-9296
E-mail: lindeboo@worldonline.nl
URL: http://www.worldonline.nl/~lindeboo

NEW ZEALAND
EBSCO NZ Ltd.
Private Mail Bag 99914
New Market
Auckland
Tel: (64 9) 524-8119
Fax: (64 9) 524-8067

NIGERIA
University Press Limited
Three Crowns Building Jericho
Private Mail Bag 5095
Ibadan
Tel: (234 22) 41-1356
Fax: (234 22) 41-2056

NORWAY
NIC Info A/S
Book Department, Postboks 6512 Etterstad
N-0606 Oslo
Tel: (47 22) 97-4500
Fax: (47 22) 97-4545

PAKISTAN
Mirza Book Agency
65, Shahrah-e-Quaid-e-Azam
Lahore 54000
Tel: (92 42) 735 3601
Fax: (92 42) 576 3714
Oxford University Press
5 Bangalore Town
Sharae Faisal
PO Box 13033
Karachi-75350
Tel: (92 21) 446307
Fax: (92 21) 4547640
E-mail: ouppak@TheOffice.net
Pak Book Corporation
Aziz Chambers 21, Queen's Road
Lahore
Tel: (92 42) 636 3222; 636 0885
Fax: (92 42) 636 2328
E-mail: pbc@brain.net.pk

PERU
Editorial Desarrollo SA
Apartado 3824, Lima 1
Tel: (51 14) 285380
Fax: (51 14) 286628

PHILIPPINES
International Booksource Center Inc.
1127-A Antipolo St, Barangay, Venezuela
Makati City
Tel: (63 2) 896 6501; 6505; 6507
Fax: (63 2) 896 1741

POLAND
International Publishing Service
Ul. Piekna 31/37
00-677 Warzawa
Tel: (48 2) 628-6089
Fax: (48 2) 621-7255
E-mail: books%ips@ikp.atm.com.pl
URL: http://www.ipscg.waw.pl/ips/export/

PORTUGAL
Livraria Portugal
Apartado 2681, Rua Do Carmo 70-74
1200 Lisbon
Tel: (1) 347-4982
Fax: (1) 347-0264

ROMANIA
Compani De Librari Bucuresti S.A.
Str. Lipscani no. 26, sector 3
Bucharest
Tel: (40 1) 613 9645
Fax: (40 1) 312 4000

RUSSIAN FEDERATION
Isdatelstvo <Ves Mir>
9a, Kolpachniy Pereulok
Moscow 101831
Tel: (7 095) 917 87 49
Fax: (7 095) 917 92 59

SINGAPORE, TAIWAN, MYANMAR, BRUNEI
Ashgate Publishing Asia Pacific Pte. Ltd.
41 Kallang Pudding Road #04-03
Golden Wheel Building
Singapore 349316
Tel: (65) 741-5166
Fax: (65) 742-9356
E-mail: ashgate@asianconnect.com

SLOVENIA
Gospodarski Vestnik Publishing Group
Dunajska cesta 5
1000 Ljubljana
Tel: (386 61) 133 83 47; 132 12 30
Fax: (386 61) 133 80 30
E-mail: repansekj@gvestnik.si

SOUTH AFRICA, BOTSWANA
For single titles:
Oxford University Press Southern Africa
Vasco Boulevard, Goodwood
P.O. Box 12119, N1 City 7463
Cape Town
Tel: (27 21) 595 4400
Fax: (27 21) 595 4430
E-mail: oxford@oup.co.za
For subscription orders:
International Subscription Service
P.O. Box 41095
Craighall
Johannesburg 2024
Tel: (27 11) 880-1448
Fax: (27 11) 880-6248
E-mail: iss@is.co.za

SPAIN
Mundi-Prensa Libros, S.A.
Castello 37
28001 Madrid
Tel: (34 1) 431-3399
Fax: (34 1) 575-3998
E-mail: libreria@mundiprensa.es
URL: http://www.mundiprensa.es/
Mundi-Prensa Barcelona
Consell de Cent, 391
08009 Barcelona
Tel: (34 3) 488-3492
Fax: (34 3) 487-7659
E-mail: barcelona@mundiprensa.es

SRI LANKA, THE MALDIVES
Lake House Bookshop
100, Sir Chittampalam Gardiner Mawatha
Colombo 2
Tel: (94 1) 32105
Fax: (94 1) 432104
E-mail: LHL@sri.lanka.net

SWEDEN
Wennergren-Williams AB
P.O. Box 1305
S-171 25 Solna
Tel: (46 8) 705-97-50
Fax: (46 8) 27-00-71
E-mail: mail@wwi.se

SWITZERLAND
Librairie Payot Service Institutionnel
Côtes-de-Montbenon 30
1002 Lausanne
Tel: (41 21) 341-3229
Fax: (41 21) 341-3235
ADECO Van Diemen EditionsTechniques
Ch. de Lacuez 41
CH1807 Blonay
Tel: (41 21) 943 2673
Fax: (41 21) 943 3605

THAILAND
Central Books Distribution
306 Silom Road
Bangkok 10500
Tel: (66 2) 235-5400
Fax: (66 2) 237-8321

TRINIDAD & TOBAGO AND THE CARRIBBEAN
Systematics Studies Ltd.
St. Augustine Shopping Center
Eastern Main Road, St. Augustine
Trinidad & Tobago, West Indies
Tel: (868) 645-8466
Fax: (868) 645-8467
E-mail: tobe@trinidad.net

UGANDA
Gustro Ltd.
PO Box 9997, Madhvani Building
Plot 16/4 Jinja Rd.
Kampala
Tel: (256 41) 251 467
Fax: (256 41) 251 468
E-mail: gus@swiftuganda.com

UNITED KINGDOM
Microinfo Ltd.
P.O. Box 3, Alton, Hampshire GU34 2PG
England
Tel: (44 1420) 86848
Fax: (44 1420) 89889
E-mail: wbank@ukminfo.demon.co.uk
URL: http://www.microinfo.co.uk

VENEZUELA
Tecni-Ciencia Libros, S.A.
Centro Cuidad Comercial Tamanco
Nivel C2, Caracas
Tel: (58 2) 959 5547; 5035; 0016
Fax: (58 2) 959 5636

ZAMBIA
University Bookshop, University of Zambia
Great East Road Campus
P.O. Box 32379
Lusaka
Tel: (260 1) 252 576
Fax: (260 1) 253 952